Reform versus Dreams

Preventing Student Failure

Rosalind LaRocque

ROWMAN & LITTLEFIELD EDUCATION
A division of
ROWMAN & LITTLEFIELD PUBLISHERS, INC.
Lanham • New York • Toronto • Plymouth, UK

Published by Rowman & Littlefield Education
A division of Rowman & Littlefield Publishers, Inc.
A wholly owned subsidiary of The Rowman & Littlefield Publishing Group, Inc.
4501 Forbes Boulevard, Suite 200, Lanham, Maryland 20706
www.rowman.com

10 Thornbury Road, Plymouth PL6 7PP, United Kingdom

British Library Cataloguing in Publication Information Available

Library of Congress Cataloging-in-Publication Data Available

ISBN 978-1-61048-735-1 (cloth : alk. paper)—ISBN 978-1-61048-736-8 (pbk. : alk. paper)—ISBN
978-1-61048-737-5 (electronic)

™
The paper used in this publication meets the minimum requirements of American
National Standard for Information Sciences Permanence of Paper for Printed Library
Materials, ANSI/NISO Z39.48-1992.

Printed in the United States of America

Contents

Foreword   v

Preface   vii

Acknowledgments   ix

1   A Call to Action   1
2   A Place to Stand   5
3   Fulfilling the Dream   19
4   The Impact of ILT   45
5   Reflections   57
6   Words of Wisdom   69
7   From Then to Now   79

Appendix A: Group Expectations Letter to Parents   83
Appendix B: Class Rules   85
Appendix C: Monthly Attendance and Grade Report   87
Appendix D : Request Form for a Parent-Teacher Conference   89
Appendix E: Collaborating with the Guidance Department   91
Appendix F: Response from the Guidance Department   93
Appendix G: Career Program Presentation Schedule   95
Appendix H: Thank You Letter to Counselors   97
Appendix I: Thank-You Letter to Presenters   99
Appendix J: Youth Multi-Service Center   101
Appendix K: Extra Credit Information   103
Appendix L: Two-Month Evaluation Results   105
Appendix M: Budget for Integrated Learning Teams   107
Bibliography   109
Index   115
About the Author   121

Foreword

Never doubt that a small group of thoughtful, committed citizens can change the world. Indeed, it's the only thing that ever has. —Margaret Mead

This is a story of school reform from the inside out. It is a profound story of what a dedicated group of teachers can do to bring about improved learning conditions for all students. By engaging in dialogue, facilitating group processes, thinking interdependently, and persisting, this group of teachers not only changed school conditions for learning, they also changed their own individual perceptions and mental models about learning.

Dating back to studies in the 1950s, teacher expectations have been shown to make a difference for learning. The 1968 classic by Robert Rosenthal and Lenore Jacobson, *Pygmalion in the Classroom: Teacher Expectation and Pupils' Intellectual Development*, asks the question: "Does how a teacher views a student shape the student?" Rosenthal and Jacobson demonstrated that teachers unwittingly create a self-fulfilling prophecy through their expectations of students. More importantly, they found that this self-fulfilling prophecy can create positive or negative results. In other words, when teachers perceive "at-risk" students as unable, incapable, failing, and unwilling learners, those students tend to fail. When teachers expect students to do well, they tend to do well.

We know that teacher expectations matter. Their ability to make a collective difference for student learning is what distinguishes excellence when comparing and evaluating schools. More recently, Carol Dweck (2004) studied how students' perceptions about intellect, whether fixed or growing, impact student achievement and that these views are shaped by the teacher's belief system. Teachers who strive to nourish growth are the ones who see the abnormalities of learners in complex classrooms as the problems to solve, not the problems to get rid of.

This day-to-day work in schools, in which educators strive to make the difference that matters, succeeds or fails based on the teacher's mental maps. Sadly the failures are what rob some children of an education. Educational leaders seeking reform from the inside out, beginning with the daily work of teachers, can seek ways to influence this mental energy by helping teachers find positive, resourceful ways to respond to their students.

This book supports the concept of Integrated Learning Teams, yet the larger story is what it takes to make those teams work—how to forge a team that shares a common vision and thinks interdependently so as to work and strive cooperatively toward desired goals. It takes commitment, persistence, skillful listening, empathy, curiosity, dedication, flexibility, and lots of knowledge. These dispositions define a sense of community. Such a group values "we-ness" more than "me-ness."

Group members are altruistic. They value consensus and are able to hold their own values and actions in abeyance in order to lend their energies and resources to the achievement of group goals. They contribute themselves to a common good, seek collegiality, and draw on the resources of others. They regard conflict as valuable, trusting their abilities to manage group differences in productive ways. They continue to learn based on feedback from others and from their consciousness of their own actions and effects on others. They seek collaborative engagement, knowing that all of us together is more efficient that any one of us.

Having a sense of community means knowing that we will benefit from participating in, contributing to, and receiving feedback from professional relationships and being willing to create and change relationships to benefit our work.

Just as interdependent persons contribute to a common good, they also draw on the resources of others. Collaborative thinkers realize the potential to significantly influence the direction of the community of which they are a part.

Education today continues to be faced with increases in critical national and social issues. As of this writing, our entire national educational system might be considered "at risk" because of such controversies as teacher evaluation, national standards and core competencies, No Child Left Behind, Race to the Top, testing, school funding, and so on.

These problems will be solved only when individuals can work in groups—such as the one described in this volume—can think together, can put the needs of students ahead of their own political ambitions, can be open and flexible, and can consider points of view other than their own. Collaborative efforts in schools today make this quality more essential than ever.

Arthur L. Costa, EdD, professor emeritus
California State University, Sacramento

Preface

In 1991, a team of high school teachers were given an opportunity to go beyond the restrictive structures of their school and create a new program aimed at providing opportunities for at-risk tenth-grade students to develop academically, emotionally, and behaviorally.

These teachers had been operating in a traditional school where all that seemed to matter was student performance measured by a single standardized test score. The curriculum was delivered, the principal evaluated the scores, and if students failed to pass the standardized test, teachers were blamed. The school then waited for someone in the district office to suggest the necessary changes and the principals, in turn, shared the information with their schools.

That year, the principal got word that sixteen students who were identified as at-risk and disruptive were coming to the school and that their presence might threaten the safety and order of the school environment. As the research would recommend, a proactive move by the principal brought five teachers together, with one facilitating the process, to develop a plan. The plan called for every question about and challenge to existing traditional structures such as the data reporting processes, bell schedules, the evaluation tool, and assessment practices to be reexamined. This work was done by teachers who had been made passive by a system that relegated teachers to be just teachers in the classroom and nothing else.

This book outlines how four teachers and a teacher-facilitator not only changed practices in the school and the classroom but how they used research as the blueprint to design the program for these potentially difficult students. Ultimately, the program served 483 students instead of just sixteen.

Although the team documented data to gauge the impact of the program, this was by no means a scientific study. However, seminal (tried and tested) research was used to scaffold the learning and social development of these students.

What was accomplished was quite an achievement and perhaps could be applied elsewhere. While every reform program has its own context, the hope here is that the reader will gain from this book the "how" — the process, the questions that need to be answered before one can design a program that can serve the needs of all children in today's schools. This book recognizes individuals and schools who have gone beyond academics and policies to support student learning.

Acknowledgments

This book is dedicated to Gustav, who advocated that this experience be shared. To Cecil, Lovely, Willie, Kent, the PTA, and the Vision Center, who had the courage to support teachers who were willing to "think outside the box" when it was unthinkable. To the teachers in the program, you made the experience possible. To the parents who supported the program and their children. To any teacher who takes on the role of teacher leader. To the local AFT, who made me aware that those unions not only fight for fairness in the workplace but also seek to support the professional development of their members to impact student learning. To members of the senate and the district, who supported this work. Special thanks to Art Costa, Ron Brandt, Heidi Jacobs, Ted Sizer, Robin Fogarty, Erick Erickson, James Bellanca, and Gordon Vars, whose work provided the foundations of the program.

ONE

A Call to Action

Every reform project has a context. In this chapter we will discuss the catalyst for the reform program that was developed. In this case, sixteen at-risk students provided the catalyst for a program aimed at ensuring their success and the security of the learning environment. The school where the reform program was implemented had a total of 2,080 students in the tenth to twelfth grade. More than half of the school population was eligible for free lunch and the average income of the families was around $45,000 per year. Overcrowding forced the school authorities to move the ninth grade to the junior high.

Overcrowding at the school had been associated with high failure rates and high levels of absenteeism. Historically, the tenth graders had been recognized for high levels of absenteeism, low test scores, and high dropout rates. In fact, it was estimated that a class of approximately 500 incoming freshmen would produce a graduating class between 275 and 300 students.

In 1991, one month before the students arrived at his school, the high school principal, a proactive instructional leader intent on supporting student learning, asked four teachers and a teacher facilitator to develop an education program for the at-risk students. The principal explained that because junior high spanned grades 7 to 9, tenth grade would be the first high school experience for these students. The limited information he had about the students indicated that they were over age, they were low performers, and exhibited irresponsible behavior. In fact, in junior high, their behavior had threatened the safety and smooth operations of the school.

The principal's goal was to develop a program that would at the very least ensure school safety by minimizing the negative behavior of these

1

students. He hoped this would, in turn, promote their academic success and improve their attitudes toward school.

The program needed to be ready for implementation when school opened in four weeks. The principal depended heavily on this group of teachers for the program's development and success. Asking teachers to develop this program demonstrated his commitment to shared leadership.

Research indicates that to ensure success, program planning of this nature should be conducted for at least a year. The program the principal requested needed to be developed within a month, calling into question the chances of its success. However, in this case, doing nothing immediately might be more costly than doing something that at least secured school safety and possibly promoted student learning.

Research models recommend starting small; only four core teachers and an additional one in a facilitator's role were involved in this program at its outset. But numbers alone do not guarantee success. In the isolated cultures that exist in many schools, it can be challenging to identify educators who have excellent interpersonal skills and a disposition that enables them to dissolve the walls of isolation and work as part of a team.

Before leaving the group to discuss options, the principal suggested that the students be distributed among the four teachers and at specific times students would be removed from their scheduled classes for social skills training with the facilitator. Although the group did not yet have a plan at this point, they determined as a team that the sixteen students should not be isolated.

Clearly, a comprehensive approach would prove more beneficial, but at this point the group did not know what that would look like. It was unusual for teachers to have a formal plan specifically for at-risk students—typically instructional adjustments were made based on the recommendations from the district's Research and Development Office. But these suggestions arrived by the end of the first quarter; too late to be effective. Cautiously, the group began exploring just what the program might entail.

Preliminary discussions revealed that the team members did not share a common language. Although the discussion was meaningful, they were not discussing from the same perspective or a common knowledge base.

The teacher facilitator had been outstanding in the school system. Services rendered included department chair, one of the first five master teachers, and now facilitator of this project. As part of the master teacher program, the district granted leave for various professional development opportunities, some of which were sponsored by the district and the local union. Areas of expertise for the facilitator included clinical supervision, system reform, and an understanding of cognitive science. During that first meeting the group established a course of action. The group agreed that the team members would meet daily; the teacher facilitator would keep the principal abreast of the group's activities through brief reports.

In preparation for the next meeting, the facilitator asked team members to identify and bring in any research on education reform that focused on at-risk or failing students. This information would support the group's development of a sound research knowledge base that would lead to an equally sound research-based program, thereby making it easier to defend its implementation. The team hoped the program would not be short-lived. If done well, it would become sustainable over the years.

To be successful, this group had to be more than a learning community; they had to be risk takers, emerging from their safe havens (their classrooms) to work collaboratively. Such structured collaboration is not common in many high schools. Rather, educators typically work alone, collaborating only when working with friends or to tackle a short, noninstructional project such as textbook adoption.

Whatever program the group conceived, it had to be intense. The students were already lagging far behind academically. Yet, this program had to incorporate more than just academics. The educational context of this program would seek to address the emotional, academic, and social needs of the students as well—areas stressed by resiliency research.

SUMMARY

There comes a time when one is forced to make a choice between existing policies and doing what is right for students. More importantly, while one is certain that something needs to be done, the stark reality is that no pre-developed program will do the work and there is nothing to purchase and implement wholesale. This was the situation in St. Cedar High School.

At the beginning of the school year, four teachers were commissioned by the principal to develop a program to address the needs of sixteen at-risk students who would be attending the school that year. That program had to be developed from the ground up and the teachers would use research to build a program that addressed the social-emotional needs of the students. In doing so, several existing district-based policies had to be adjusted to support the program that the teachers would develop.

TWO

A Place to Stand

In this chapter we will discuss the team's journey as they tried to find the best research on which to build the program. As requested, team members brought to the next meeting—and subsequent meetings—research about education reform that focused on at-risk or failing students and hoped it might guide the program design. From this point on, research findings drove the discussions throughout the development process, with the facilitator offering a framework for initial discussions about the program. Each piece of research would be reviewed to determine its possible contribution to the program.

The team began by reviewing the Secretary's Commission on Achieving Necessary Skills (SCANS) Report, from the U.S. Labor Department. Then, the *A Nation at Risk* report from the U.S. Department of Education prompted them to expand the goal of their work from simply developing a program to ensure school safety and academic success to also preparing all students for the world of work.

The SCANS Report cited five major areas in which students lacked preparation. These areas were:

Resources: allocating time, money, materials, space, and staff

Interpersonal Skills: working on teams, teaching others, serving customers, leading, negotiating, and working well with people from culturally diverse backgrounds

Information: acquiring and evaluating data, organizing and maintaining files, interpreting and communicating, and using computers to process information

Systems: understanding social, organizational, and technological systems, monitoring and correcting performance, and designing or improving systems

Technology: selecting equipment and tools, applying technology to specific tasks, and maintaining and troubleshooting technologies

The areas that stood out for the team were time management, communication, interpersonal skills, and technological skills. Except for technology, these skills were not new; however, little time was devoted to teaching these skills explicitly. In recent times, though, technology has created a presence in education whereby many students can be instructed using the Internet and now online courses and degrees are available for students and adults.

The SCANS Report also highlighted the importance of technology skills. Those skills include the ability to select equipment and tools, apply technology to specific tasks, and maintain and troubleshoot technologies. Technology was extremely limited at the high school during the time this program was being developed. The school had one computer teacher who taught five classes; the curriculum was restricted to proficiency in the use of Microsoft Word. The resources to sustain a technology class of the magnitude outlined in the SCANS Report were nonexistent, so for the team, the library became a focal point for the program, serving as a source of information and a resource to connect students to content.

The SCANS Report prompted deep reflection from the team; a connection between behavior and a lack of skills seemed possible. The question then was, could the lack of preparation for the world elicit the negative behavior at-risk students exhibited? Were students noncompliant because they saw no connection between their world and what they were being asked to do in school? The team decided that the employability skills outlined in SCANS—in addition to the completion of coursework— would be at the core of the program.

The other document, *A Nation at Risk*, also addressed the levels of proficiency of American students. According to this document, published in 1983, America's students were trailing behind international students in almost all subjects. If the goal was to prepare students for the world of work, then catering to just sixteen students was not only a bad approach but a waste of resources.

The team began brainstorming ideas about what the program would look like or entail. After reading the book, *The School as a Home for the Mind* by Arthur Costa (1991), the team examined six questions that would be considered as the program was being developed. The team members discussed each question with the goal of framing a response that would help identify components of the program.

1. WHAT DO YOU KNOW ABOUT THE STUDENTS?

The first question posed centered on knowing the students. Because the team did not have a lot of information about the sixteen students, they discussed what they needed to know to be successful in helping these students. What information they did have led them to conclude that the students fell within similar socioeconomic brackets that made them eligible to attend this public school. Because the students' records were confidential, the teachers would have to get to know them as the year progressed.

The team knew well that too often innovations and programs are developed based solely on test scores, without considering extraneous factors. Sometimes successful programs are implemented wholesale without the necessary adjustments to support their effectiveness in the environment in which they will be used.

One source of information related to this challenge came from the facilitator who had attended a workshop presented by Gordon Vars at the 1990 Association of Supervision and Curriculum Development (ASCD) annual conference. Vars contended that relevant adjustments should be made to the curriculum to engage students and promote clear connections to their world and their needs. As a result, student behavior would improve. He also supported the premise that, if the curriculum did not change, educators could still make instruction and content meaningful for students, but that educators first had to *know* their students (Vars, 1978).

A ten-question survey Vars provided during his ASCD workshop served as the foundation for getting to know the goals and aspirations of the students in the program. The program would enlist as many tenth-grade students as possible. The survey began with the usual questions about demographics. Students were then asked about their likes (e.g., hobbies, favorite subject, and favorite types of books), interests, and career of choice in the next ten years. The survey also asked students about their pet peeves, how they handled anger, if they had any experience being bullied, teacher actions they disliked, their most disliked subject, and reasons for noncompletion of homework.

The questionnaire served two purposes: It forced students to reflect on their lives, goals, and aspirations and the steps they needed to achieve those goals and it enabled the educators to get to know the students a little better. Knowing students beyond ID numbers and labels (e.g., at-risk) allows educators to design learning opportunities that connect school and personal goals. However, not all goals are based on test scores. Goals can include changing learner behaviors or attitudes toward school.

The question on the survey that really resonated with the team was the one that asked students to reveal where they saw themselves in ten years. They used the responses to this question to create a career course to connect content to career ambitions. Based on this finding, the team unanimously agreed that the curriculum should be used as a vehicle to prepare students for life rather than just for passing the Terra Nova, the standardized test administered at the time.

In the hope of understanding the at-risk child, the team decided to explore what the research had to say about students who were labeled as such. Erik Erikson (1983) identified the general characteristics of at-risk students. Including a need to belong and to learn in a cooperative environment, these students had a tendency to drop out of school as a result of seeing no connection between education and the quality of their life in the future.

Ironically, at-risk students crave social connections but are shunned because of their behavior. Thus, the students who would participate in the program had been identified as a group of students who exhibited antisocial behavior but who might actually yearn to belong.

Erikson's findings were a major breakthrough for the team members, because they could establish that at-risk students wanted schools and classrooms that were nurturing and provided a sense of community. Equally important was providing these students with a sense of purpose and a sense that those educators cared—critical in building the self-efficacy of these students. Therefore, teaching needed to go way beyond content and curriculum if the goal was to prepare students for a successful life.

All of this could not be accomplished if affective and social needs were not addressed in the classroom and in the school. The team saw the curriculum as a vehicle to help students understand their life and ability levels. The research the team examined repeatedly suggested such an approach. So they drafted a plan to make assignments serve as a means to better understand the world as well as prepare for the standardized tests. Now the revised goal was to attach a world-related assignment where natural intersections occurred in course content.

As the team members reviewed available resources, they were forced to reflect on the organizational structure and operations of the school itself. The stark realization was that the existing school culture was one of isolation—a culture in which all of the teachers had operated for years.

Now the task was to remove the walls of isolation and create a team in a family-type environment so these students could succeed. Those engaged in the program had to become learners and change agents for a system that had failed to meet the needs of some of its students.

2. WHAT SHOULD THE STRUCTURE OF
THE CURRICULUM LOOK LIKE?

Undoubtedly, the curriculum had to include the skills cited in the SCANS Report. Because no structured curriculum existed at the time, the scope and sequence supported by the textbook served as the curriculum. The goal then became to review the scope and sequence to determine *What's Worth Teaching* (Brady, 1989), a consideration many researchers have examined.

According to Ted Sizer (1984), determining what is essential establishes an "essential curriculum." From Sizer's work, the team understood the importance of creating an essential curriculum (identifying the most important concepts of the course) while accommodating annual state education mandates and still addressing academics and social problems. The team confirmed the importance of a strong connection between curriculum and instruction.

Since the 1990s, two sets of standards have been developed. Recently, a set of Common Core State Standards for reading and math (www.corestandards.org) has been released. This was a joint effort by the Council of Chief State School Officers and the National Governors Association, and the AFT was invited to assist. This was an attempt to improve the common understanding by all involved in education about what all children should be able to do at every grade level. Now the work begins to put them in a language that students can understand and more importantly, to align curriculum and testing with the standards and curriculum.

3. HOW IS INSTRUCTION DELIVERED?

In considering this question, several truths were evident: Students have varying needs, so instruction should not be all lectures but a more facilitative approach. In addition, the content should be used to teach academic and life skills, drawing connections between the content and the students' world. A survey of the research offered a strategy for combining content and skill while making school relevant to the real world.

Heidi Hayes Jacobs's (1989) resources provided significant guidance in this approach to instruction. Although Jacobs's work provided a way to think about the curriculum structure, existing models were not appropriate for the context. The framework used to integrate lessons focused on themes; the team's program required that thinking skills be the focus. The plan for the team's program then was to integrate thinking and life skills into the lesson design.

Because instruction was at the heart of the program, the team discussed at length the role thinking would play in the curriculum and, more important, how it would be taught. How could they integrate content and still be able to teach skills and relevance to world events? Robin Fogarty's (1991) *threaded* model allowed for such an integration of life and critical thinking skills to be woven through the four core content areas, serving as the backdrop to an activity that involved a world event. Robin Fogarty's (1991) *threaded* model allowed not only life skills and critical-thinking skills to be woven through the four core subject areas but facilitated a smooth transition to an extended activity on real-world problems that required the use of thinking skills. This approach enabled students to use thinking skills as a mechanism to solve problems.

Although the team ultimately settled on the *threaded* model as the instructional framework, as with everything, there is always a word of caution. Jacobs's (1989) caution focused on the concept of *forced fit*. During such times when the skill does not work for all content, it should not be included in the particular lesson design. Jacobs also cautioned about relying on a "potpourri" (i.e., "simply juxtaposing several disciplines") approach to curriculum development (p. 2).

Team members understood the need for balanced, cohesive lessons designed to help students draw from the range of subject matter in order to serve specific needs. This meant, for example, that textbook chapters might not always be sequenced.

The team determined that effectively integrated lessons should create learning continuity and be explicit about connections between the concepts the students are taught. Each discipline field-based lesson would be built on an essential question that enabled an understanding of the content while promoting connections between concepts and the infusion of interdisciplinary experiences. Such lessons foster thinking, include behavioral indicators of attitudinal change, and allow for a solid evaluation process.

Therefore, the team decided, skills highlighted in the previous year's annual report on student performance, which clearly indicated areas needing improvement, would be infused in the lessons. Essay writing and thinking were areas of particularly low performance. Surely teaching students to think beyond their innate abilities was critical.

At this point the framework for the program was beginning to take shape. The survey would provide the means to know the students. A career-preparation program would be built from the responses to the career question included on the survey. The lesson design would use the threaded model to support the teaching of thinking and life skills and connect content to world experiences through engaging activities. When possible, using the threaded model, thinking and life skills would be infused into the lessons while teachers provided scaffolds to help students achieve the identified goals.

4. HOW WOULD THE PROGRAM BE ASSESSED?

This question asked change agents to determine how programs hoping to effect change would be assessed. In considering this question, Ron Brandt's (1998) work drove the discussion to include concepts such as objectives and incremental evaluation steps. Successful reform programs identified incremental goals which are articulated as objectives. These objectives served as a means for gauging the program's progress. Programs such as the one the team was developing could use artifacts such as tests, projects, responses to essay questions, and performance-based assignments to gauge success.

Other indicators of success would include nonacademic goals. In fact, Erikson (1983) and Brandt (1998) both highlighted the importance of non-academic goals (e.g., attendance, individual well-being) as supports for student learning. They determined that a change in learner behavior could positively affect goal setting and the achievement of career aspirations. However, change does not come about by merely tweaking. Rather, it comes by setting benchmarks, gathering data, and engaging in the processes of reflection and infusing adjustments—tasks based on data gathered during implementation.

The team defined the data to be gathered to assess the impact of the program. Students' classwork, formative assessments, end-of-year grades, attendance, attitudinal changes toward school, and the level of parent engagement would all be indicators of success or areas of improvement. Attendance rates and homework completion also would be included.

All aspects of the program would be evaluated. Informal evaluations would provide ongoing feedback but the final evaluation would be based on how well students did on the departmental exams administered at the end of the year. The midterm would be considered a formative assessment. The evaluations would be comprehensive, including nonacademic indicators as well.

Students' classwork, formative assessments, semester grades, attendance and attitudinal changes toward school, referral records, and the level of parent engagement paved the way for defining the objectives for the program. These objectives were to improve student learning, improve performance on standardized tests, increase levels of parent involvement, develop self-improvement and time management skills, and improve teacher practice through professional development.

5. HOW SHOULD THE PROFESSIONAL DEVELOPMENT PLAN BE STRUCTURED IN ORDER TO MEET THE NEEDS OF THE EDUCATORS AND STUDENTS?

Professional development is a significant component because change has to be sustained and successful programs require an abundance of knowledge and training. Indeed, this question brought professional development into the discussion. Memberships to education organizations such as ASCD, subscriptions to professional publications such as *Education Leadership* and *Phi Delta Kappan*, and district professional development offerings or an occasional national conference summed up the professional growth opportunities for educators.

Yet research is clear, professional development cannot be absent from reform models. Everyone involved must have an opportunity to experience growth. Costa (1991) underscored this philosophy by asking change agents to consider how the professional development plan should be structured in order to meet the needs of the teachers and students. In short, the program had to benefit both, because in environments of change, both students and educators are learners.

Brandt's (1998) work provided the team with a concept of a learning organization. According to Brandt, effective learning organizations understand that no program is static; such programs require constant evaluation and feedback from all stakeholders, particularly those whom the program serves. Several of these factors had already been considered. Brandt's recommendations simply served to verify the team's approach and to highlight the importance of gathering data. Peter Kline and Bernard Saunders (2010) outline similar characteristics of learning organizations in their book titled, *Ten Steps to a Learning Organization.*

6. WHAT DO SCHOOLS AND CLASSROOMS NEED TO RECEIVE EDUCATION REFORM PROGRAMS?

The last question the team examined led them to consider what conditions needed to be in place for the program to be implemented. To respond to this question, the team members discussed systems and factors in the school or district that did not optimize student success. The brainstormed list included the following items:

- Absenteeism/class-cutting
- No connection between what is learned in school and life
- A lack of opportunity for educators to be creative
- Late release of standardized test results
- One-size-fits-all approach
- Lack of parent involvement

- An absence of active, energizing classroom instruction and projects
- Lack of time
- Lack of skills such as time management
- Little emphasis on thinking skills, too much emphasis on the level of a question
- Absence of instruction in life skills that support personal growth
- Inadequate meaningful professional development
- Noncompletion of homework
- Need for structural and policy changes (e.g., schedules and progress reports)

Six broad categories emerged from this brainstorm: curriculum, instruction, professional development, necessary life skills (attendance, homework completion, and time management), parent involvement, and time.

With regard to life skills, the team turned its attention to the conditions that had to be considered during the program design. At the time, the available resources did not address attendance beyond the fact that poor attendance negatively affected learning. Since then, Hedy Chang (2010) has conducted a detailed study of the impact of nonattendance in grades K–3; but both middle and high schools experience the impact of poor attendance or excessive excuses for being absent. More information can be found on her website, *Attendance Works* (www.attendanceworks. org/qa).

The team members discussed the issue of attendance. One explanation for the high absenteeism rates was the layout of the school campus. The school was spread out and the fencing did not enclose the entire perimeter. Even where it did, the fence was not always intact.

Sizer's (1984) concept of "school-within-a-school" provided the idea for the program: to ensure that the classrooms for the four subject areas were located next to each other and to give teachers common planning time. Having the classrooms within close proximity would give the team more control over attendance because student movement between the core subject areas would be confined to these classes. Besides, conversations among the team members during common planning time made it easy to readily identify students with attendance patterns and truant behavior.

Toward the end of the twentieth century, Robert Cannady and Michael Rettig (1995) proposed block scheduling as a catalyst for change in high schools. The process allowed students to focus on fewer subjects during a semester and when implemented correctly yielded amazing results. One downfall was instruction remaining the same for the ninety-minute as it was for the fifty-five-minute class. As a result, students deemed school boring. The team adopted the idea of block scheduling but relegated the meaning to students moving in blocks (en bloc) between classes. This would create small communities by period and subject.

With regard to homework, the team agreed that homework assignments had to provide opportunities for practice and serve as the liaison between content and the students' world. The resources on homework articulated that assignments should not be given unless students had mastered the content. Such claims gave the team reason to pause, as every homework mandate imposed by the district or the school stressed the need to give assignments every night. Such a directive dictated that students complete assignments on concepts for which they had not achieved a deep understanding.

The research also suggested that unless the homework assignments are at the same level of difficulty as the content recently covered in class, assigning homework is counterproductive. Thus, the team members determined that homework would be assigned first and foremost for practice on material studied and then to promote connections to the world through project-based assignments. The team knew they would need buy-in from the principal. If there was resistance, the team planned to argue that Project-Based Learning (PBL) was initiated in the late 1960s in the health sciences at McMaster University and later it had been adopted by other medical school programs as well as education.

Time for collaboration was essential but did not exist during the regular school day. Again, they would need support from the principal to suspend certain district mandates. Sizer's (1984) "school-within-a-school" model provided a framework for addressing the time issue.

With four classes, the contractually agreed upon planning period, and an additional common planning time, much of the needed collaboration and the additional administrative duties that such a program demanded would get done. In addition, common planning time would promote parent engagement. Team members could engage parents in the process during common planning time, discuss absenteeism and class-cutting, and include professional development activities for the team.

With regards to scheduling, math and science classes would be sequenced, as would language arts and social studies. This meant that period 1 in language arts would be with period 2 in social studies. Similarly, period 2 social studies would be with period 1 language arts. Such sequencing allowed for language arts/social studies to be grouped, for example, to view a movie during one class period instead of over an entire week.

Many school-based reform agents step up without receiving additional compensation for their work. This was certainly the case with this team. Although this program was a school-based effort, common planning time and adjustments to the homework policy required amendments to existing contractual agreements. The local union was supportive; the facilitator/master teacher training had been cosponsored by the district and union, but these requests for the program went beyond the contract.

Requests for changes of this magnitude required justification. The team outlined the reasons for these changes to present to the principal. For example, the row of classrooms would help curb truancy by permitting students to be monitored in a controlled environment and common planning would ensure time to develop lessons, participate in professional development activities, and meet with parents as a team.

One of the major goals of the program was to have the students not only obtain good grades but also change their perspective on life in general. According to the resources the teachers reviewed, students who received counseling beyond academics exceeded expectations. Such counseling would include areas such as career goals, home conditions, life, and perhaps just having someone to talk to—especially when it came to post-graduation plans.

The importance of receiving counseling beyond academics was highlighted in the work of R. L. Bednar and S. L. Weinberg who, in 1970, reviewed twenty-three studies that evaluated the effectiveness of different programs for low-achieving students. D. S. Kirscenbaum and M. G. Perri (1982) subsequently reviewed an additional thirty-three studies. In both instances, the researchers concluded that students stood a better chance of success if they received counseling in conjunction with academic studies.

Providing counseling beyond academics required the assistance of the guidance department staff, who would be asked to function in ways not outlined in their contracts. A request to the counselors asked that the rule restricting college fairs to upperclassmen be waived. Allowing the tenth graders in the program to attend college fairs, chaperoned by their teachers, would support the career program by helping students work toward a goal.

The role of stakeholders in the success of reform programs is discussed extensively in the research. Beyond the four teachers, the stakeholders included the guidance counselors, the school monitors, cafeteria workers, custodial workers, and members of the business community. The school nurse and the parents were also included. Each stakeholder had a role to play and the team would partner with each one in a manner that proved beneficial to the students.

For example, the team envisaged the school monitors keeping a watchful eye on the sixteen students on the school grounds. The custodial workers would teach the students about keeping their environment clean. Members of the business community would help connect school and the students' world. If community businesses agreed, the team intended to add jobs at Christmas and the summer as components of the program. A student's access to the jobs would be dependent on grades.

The existing educational system had always involved stakeholders in a very rigid process that did not secure buy-in or commitment—or even a collaborative relationship. In fact, the invitation for involvement of stakeholders seemed more like a call to duty. The school's expectations with regard to parent involvement were that they were responsible to attend PTA meetings, show up for report cards, and sponsor or support bake sales or activities that require labor-intensive commitments. When necessary, a parent would be invited to serve on the accreditation committee. Joyce Epstein (2001) highlighted the role of partnerships between school, parents, and the community and Neal Glasgow and Paula Whitney (2008) offered advice on how to involve parents.

However, research indicates that successful teams must create an atmosphere for buy-in among all stakeholders. It is important for these identified stakeholders to become part of the educational design and play a vital role in helping students attain nonacademic goals. Parents who become cosupporters of any reform program should work with the guidance department to begin planning post–high school education as early as the tenth grade. The business community should help mold the next generation of employees. For the team, such supports were found to be what ensured the success of the program at the school.

Usually, the word *team* has been used loosely to define a group working on a project. These teams assemble for short-lived projects (e.g., textbook adoption) and then disperse once the project or mission is completed. However, teams serving as change agents should view the group's activities as ongoing and sustainable over time in order to support student learning.

Successful teams have certain unique characteristics. In addition to having a common knowledge base and resources, supportive structures must also be available, and teachers must have time to practice as long-held beliefs about teaching and learning undergo change. Cognitive science research has affirmed that mastery of any skill requires extensive practice, no matter what the skill. Posner and Raichle (1997) believed that fifteen minutes of practice daily would speed up a learner's proficiency of the skill being learned. But support is also important.

Changes in schools thrive in a supportive school culture. One challenge for the team was that this program would be embedded in a host school whose culture was still based on isolationism and competition. The team quickly cultivated a humane environment, warm relationships, and a plan to implement a job-embedded professional development structure. Research suggested that the most effective support systems for educators occur when they are comprised of other practitioners like themselves.

In recent years, several works have stressed the need to craft strategies for at-risk students. David Snow (2005) suggests several strategies in his book *Classroom Strategies for Helping At-Risk Students*. In addition, a few teachers came to the conclusion that school as is could not meet the needs of all students. In his book *Work Hard. Be Nice: How Two Inspired Teachers Created the Most Promising Schools in America*, Jay Mathews (2009) describes how two teachers envisioned another structure for schools. The message is clear: school must change.

The research described most schools as places where educators faced 200 or more students daily and opted to assign work that did not seem to push deep thinking. Students moved between classes daily, rarely having time to be immersed in any topic. The team projected that four classes with the contractual number of students or even more would create an ideal group. The program would serve the sixteen students who were the catalyst for its inception but it would also take as many students in the tenth grade that scheduling could make possible. More importantly, the instruction and learning activities in the program would strive to engage and energize the students. While moving between classes students would not feel isolated since the students would be in the same group, almost like a community.

To create an appropriate title for the program, the team focused on words that described the program—namely, *integrated* and *learning*. Ultimately the goal was to be a learning organization. After much discussion, and with influence from Brandt's and Fogarty's concepts, the team agreed on the title Integrated Learning Teams (ILT) for the program. ILT would function as an open system, being sensitive to the internal and external environment while considering the social, political, and economic conditions in which it operated.

As team members became learners acquiring new knowledge and functioning as change agents for a system that failed to meet the needs of some of its students, ongoing support from both the facilitator and principal was critical.

SUMMARY

Effective programs for at-risk students are built on seminal research. The date of the research is significant but more important is the question, does it work? The research that the team used helped define instruction, curriculum, and outlined the needs of at-risk students. These would be at the foundation of the program. Schools-within-Schools research (Sizer, 1984) was adopted by a number of very large high schools. Readers can view the list of schools in Sizer's Coalition of Essential Schools at www.essentialschools.org/affiliates. The research has made it clear that there will be some children who will not perform their best in such large environments. Given limited access to money, researchers like Sizer suggested that small schools be created within the large ones.

The team used this concept and added on the block movement between classes. The ILT approach tells us that schools will not find the answer in one study. As soon as a need is addressed it either supports or aggravates something else to which one must attend. What the team did was just that. They reviewed the studies and used the ones that best suited the learning environment they were aiming to create.

The instruction was based on the integrated model known as the threaded model. Such an approach allowed the instruction of skills to be assimilated into the content. Besides, in order to address making learning relevant to life, projects were assigned based on the skill. The project assignment was focused on world events. The structure of the assignments was designed to include the skills outlined in the SCANS Report. The goal was to make students achieve and be knowledgeable and prepared to join and contribute to the working force as well-developed citizens.

THREE
Fulfilling the Dream

This chapter explains the components of Integrated Learning Teams (ILT) and the supporting research. ILT was built on the fundamentals of research studies that aligned with the program's components. ILT did not focus on one aspect, for example, instruction, but encompassed all components to create a total program. These components are: program structure; knowing the clients; curriculum, instruction and lesson design; examples of the threaded model lesson design; a word on assessment; parents as partners and academic, career, and life skills. Program challenges and funding are also addressed.

Lionel Elvin (1977) described the shortcomings of content delivery during the traditional school day in this way: "When you are out walking, nature does not confront you for three-quarters of an hour only with flowers and in the next only with animals" (p. 29). Elvin's thoughts provided a compelling reason to consider implementing the *threaded model* lesson design, to give students a more holistic view of the content. Then the goal of ILT was to use content, the school setting, activities that support learning, and the development of life skills that made students successful in life and in their community.

If this was the main goal, then one of the components, the lesson design and method of instruction, would play a critical role. ILT was based on a philosophy that school is a place where educators use content to prepare students for life and to teach them how to think critically. The academic success that is gained allows for a smooth transition from high school to post–high school academics. The components of ILT were aligned to the needs of the at-risk students for whom the program was developed.

PROGRAM STRUCTURE

The structure of ILT included four core teachers who would share 483 students, not just the initial sixteen students the principal was concerned about. These were randomly selected students from the incoming sophomores and from those who had to repeat the tenth grade. Normally, class size allows for a maximum of twenty-seven students. However, ILT classes allowed a maximum of up to thirty-two students in an effort to relieve the strain on the other teachers since ILT staff had four classes instead of the contractual five.

Both student and teacher needs were placed at the core of the program. Several aspects of ILT challenged existing educational policy. For example, ILT advocated for assigning homework when it clearly supported learning rather than simply complying with district mandates to assign homework every night. Also, ILT sought to waive the restriction on tenth graders attending college fairs.

Most notably, the team decided that feedback was a crucial and essential component in the learning process. In terms of feedback, instructors were required to offer specific and constructive criticisms on the designed feedback form. For example, vague comments on an essay such as "well done" were not appropriate in ILT. Specific comments should include remarks on the accuracy of topic sentences and organizational alignment between the paper and its thesis statement and so on. Students also received rubrics that clearly outlined the quality of work that was considered excellent. Research confirms that students do well when they know the expectations.

Room location changed in ILT. Traditionally, wings in the school were created by subject and grade, but not in ILT. The newly established classrooms for ILT were adjacent to each other and the students moved together, helping create a family-type community setting for at-risk students and a process aimed at minimizing truancy. Table 3.1 illustrates how the students moved between classes.

Table 3.1 shows the teachers denoted by letters and the courses taught, as well as the schedules for four students (Jane, Sally, Matt, and Heather). For example, Jane goes to Educator A—language arts for the

Table 3.1.   ILT Student Class Schedules

Educators	Period 1	Period 2	Period 3	Period 4
A—Language Arts	Jane	Sally	Matt	Heather
B—Social Studies	Sally	Jane	Heather	Matt
C—Math	Matt	Heather	Jane	Sally
D—Science	Heather	Matt	Sally	Jane

first period. During second period she goes to Educator B—social studies. Sally attends social studies first period and language arts second period.

Note that Jane and Sally are "paired" throughout the schedule, allowing some collaboration between classes and subjects. For example, if Educator A—language arts wants to show *The Diary of Anne Frank* during first period and Educator B—social studies is teaching a unit on World War II, the classes can be combined into one block so Sally and Jane's class will be together for two periods.

When educators needed extra class time to complete in-depth lesson plans, they could trade periods with other instructors. Later in the week, Educator B could keep Jane's group for two periods and Educator A could keep Sally's group for two periods. Every aspect of the program was research-based and designed to provide a family setting, curb truancy, and use time more efficiently.

A key asset for ILT was the shared planning period the core educators gained. The plan was for them to work individually during the contractual "free" period and conduct collaborative planning during sixth period. The sixth period time would be used to discuss program concerns such as instruction, attendance, and academic progress. Attendance was critical to ILT's goal of turning students around and it was one of the indicators of success for the program.

During the common planning time, one of the tasks was to identify students in ILT with truant behavior. Students in ILT had to be held accountable. Together the educators developed interventions. The very next morning, students were asked for a reason for their truant behavior, in every class. If a parental conference was necessary it could be held during the common planning time—another example of the benefits of a shared planning time.

The shared time also allowed the education team to engage in professional development. Sometimes the facilitator would conduct training and several consultants were brought in to help the team become more proficient in numerous areas. Robin Fogarty's did training on the threaded model of curriculum integration and Sandra Parks did training on infusing critical thinking into the curriculum. The group also scheduled two other sessions. A concept like paper geometry helped those with a low budget acquire a geometry-type manipulative using paper and a scissors. On the other hand, the Bay Area Writing Project shared ways to scaffold writing.

The team decided that professional development would be ongoing and embedded into the daily routine. A lack of professional development could affect the program's structure; what could the team do that was meaningful if professional development was taken out of the equation? Whenever possible, team members would attend training sessions, off-campus and on-campus. In one way or another, the group would be engaged in continued professional development, improving the instructional skills that would benefit students and contribute to the success of ILT.

The facilitator conducted various training sessions aimed at strengthening the program structure; yes, classroom interactions could affect the program itself. So behaviors that could negatively influence the classroom environments were discussed very early, while building the program. A large part of the teacher behavioral research came from Jacob Kounin's (1970) work. It was important that educators in ILT recognize and analyze behaviors that negatively affected student learning and have a management plan to minimize the effect on learning.

For example, when interruptions occur as a result of the intercom or someone coming to the door, how could the teacher lessen the effect of this action while attempting to regain the students' attention? These are the type of discussions that would also be held during common planning time. What about instructional actions by the teacher that they may not be aware of? The practice of calling on one student while another student takes time to respond affects the morale of that student for whom the educator did not practice "wait time." Worse yet is giving unclear instructions that cost time spent asking for clarity.

Moreover, how will the instructor assess the effect of the pacing of the lesson on students' rate of learning? And how will student's lack of understanding be addressed without holding others back? When students' rates of learning are not considered, these students, because of their inability to follow along, sometimes resort to disruptive behavior in the classroom that distracts students around them.

Distractions also occur when the instructor begins a lesson and, in the middle of instruction, interjects something totally unrelated, short circuiting students' thinking processes. ILT educators were cautioned about the effect of these types of counterproductive behaviors and were conditioned to note the distracters and have a plan in place to avoid any adverse effect on learning.

KNOWING THE PROGRAM'S CLIENTS

It is important to know the clients for whom the program or intervention is being designed. Gordon Vars's questionnaire from the 1990 ASCD conference, which is based on his book *Interdisciplinary Teaching in the Middle Grades* (1978), offered a medium that allowed program developers to understand and get to know the students better without breaching privacy. Of the ten questions asked, one question asked about future careers and provided insight on how to connect school and academics in each student's life in a practical and meaningful way. The response to this question was crucial in the development of ILT's career component and served as the bedrock of the career component of the program.

A recurring concern throughout the research literature was that at-risk students did not care about their work, yet at the same time, other research indicated that these students had a yearning to belong. Reform agents need to recognize that these emotions and behaviors are just as important as academics in education. Note that these insecurities and vulnerabilities need to be addressed in order to achieve success in education. Therefore, the goal of ILT was to make these students feel that they belonged and that they were adequate to complete the assignments given.

ILT promoted social outings to recognize and emphasize the importance of social aspects of the learning environments for students. Some activities encouraged nurturing relationships that would develop trust and care. Such activities were movie nights and picnics. (Participation required parental permission.) Additionally, there would be a month-long academic requirement in order to be eligible to participate in these social outings.

ILT intended to support student-teacher relations by recognizing birthday and cultural celebrations in classes. These activities would help deepen bonds between teacher and student and enhance the classroom environment. The ILT team sought to understand the social environment of their students. To accomplish this, the team would reach out to the families in an emotional way by honoring special holidays celebrated by the cultures of the students in the classroom and the community.

For example, each year one cultural group observed a day to celebrate their coexistence with other cultures in the country. The team honored all cultural groups in celebration of diversity and cultural heritage. ITL proved that language and culture created no barriers.

But academics mean nothing to students who do not eat healthy or who may be in danger of being undernourished by not eating the right foods. Several students came to school without breakfast. The team planned to use the assistance of the nurse to discuss healthy eating and encourage the students to partake of the breakfast and lunch served daily in the cafeteria. To encourage the students, the teachers in ILT ate in the cafeteria hoping to alleviate any stigma about eating in the lunch room.

CURRICULUM, INSTRUCTION, AND LESSON DESIGN

Research supports the fact that reform projects aimed at developing students' thinking skills should focus on lesson design and instruction that connect students to their world, while teaching employable skills for the workplace. When connecting school to the real world, the curriculum must include important learning and life skills. It is important, then, to ensure not only a deep understanding of the content, but also to challenge students to use that content to foster thinking, problem solving, and teamwork for cooperative learning instructional models.

Barry Zimmerman, Albert Bandura, and Manuel Martinez-Pons (1992) characterized a high-achieving student as one who can delineate important information from the material at hand by underlining or highlighting pertinent information. This was the type of high-achieving students ILT hoped to produce. ILT enlisted the services of John Swann, a former teacher of Detroit Public Schools (DPS), to help students apply the skill of delineating important information by providing training for the PSATs and SATs. According to the researchers, this skill supports the methodical review of content for exams, ensuring the information will reside in the long-term memory.

A fundamental learning skill emphasized in the ILT curriculum was note taking. This is a skill designed to foster a student's deep understanding of the content as well as text structures. However, most note-taking assignments elicit four words of instruction from instructors: "read and take notes." Directions such as these are unfocused, lack clarity, and do not engage students. In fact, students simply reproduce the text they read to comply with the assignment. This reproduction of content does not foster or support deeper understanding of the content or engagement in the thinking process.

ILT curriculum would require note-taking skills to first learn the content but also become familiar with the structure of the text. For example, if the structure of the passage is one of persuasion, the directions for the assignment would ask students to take notes in the following manner: find the main argument and outline the supporting points. When note taking is done in this manner, students are able to identify and distinguish text structure; those who need more support would be instructed to use graphic organizers as an effective way to compile their notes.

During the process of note taking, the learner uses skills in summarizing and paraphrasing—two cognitive processes that help determine a person's level of contextual understanding. These skills were emphasized in the curriculum and in the lessons. Students would learn that summarizing requires the author's voice and paraphrasing requires their own voice.

Lev Vygotsky (1978) explained the journey of becoming an expert learner as one in which students move from well-structured tasks to less-structured tasks. For example, a well-structured task requires more detailed, often step-by-step instructions for students and involves thinking along with the application of basic skills. Less structured tasks are open-ended. ILT assignments considered the concept of well structured to less structured.

John Bruer's (1993) synthesis of cognitive research implied the significance of observing how "novice" students approach tasks in comparison to "expert" ones. Teachers in ILT would use this theory to assign projects with varying difficulty levels based on targeted and identified student proficiency levels. Teachers would provide additional scaffolding for students as necessary to help foster "expert" learning. Such an approach has similarities with a more recent approach titled differentiated instruction, which strives to meet students at their levels of understanding.

Moving students from more- to less-structured tasks requires scaffolds; for example, prompts and questions or cues help students attain mastery level. As students become more proficient, these scaffolds may be slowly withdrawn. These concepts were all part of the curriculum in ILT. Additionally, the curriculum required that assessment checklists and rubrics accompany all assignments so students could have an outline of the quality of work expected.

The purpose of schools, according to Sizer (1984), is to help students use their minds. Therefore, strategies for developing critical thinking would be integrated into the curriculum. ILT would be a skill-based curriculum where content would be used to teach these skills. The goal was to prepare students for life, not to simply pass state assessments and other tests.

Students in ILT would be taught to think critically about content and its application in the real world using the skills identified in the threaded design model. Assignments were distributed to students with the expectation that they would demonstrate understanding by applying concepts to life rather than simply regurgitating content.

Developing the concept of thinking brings Bloom's taxonomy to the center of the ILT curriculum. In his work, Bloom (1987) defined varying levels of tasks by which he could assess the progress of the students with special needs with whom he was working. Researchers of cognitive science stress that before students are required to respond to questions, they must know and understand the content needed to answer the question. This kind of research challenges the traditional hierarchical classification of questions as high- or low-order. The emphasis should not be on the level of question but rather on the content of the question: what is being asked and how the material should be delivered and taught in order to get the desired response from the learner. In the end, it is just a question. That would be the focus of ILT's curriculum.

This debate about Bloom's taxonomy being labeled as high or low level and categorized by question types (analysis, evaluation, etc.) has continued throughout the twentieth century. Maureen Donohue-Smith spoke about Bloom's Model in the *Chronicle Review* in 2006:

> In using Bloom's model, however, a caveat is in order. Bloom and other scholars did not consider one category of question superior to another, but people often assume that more-complex, "higher order" questions are intrinsically better than simple fact-seeking ones. We should avoid such a hierarchical interpretation of the categories, thinking instead of them as arranged in a feedback loop. (p. 1)

Noting these understandings, ILT planned to use questioning as one of the ways to assess student learning. Therefore, students would be taught how to use all of Bloom's Taxonomy to craft responses rather than get consumed with labeling questions by type prior to crafting the response. That students know and understand the material must be a given before they are expected to respond to questions. During instruction, ILT educators would assure that students can effectively repackage information to respond to a question. Students' proficiency will be demonstrated when they can demonstrate that they have the basic knowledge, or facts, and know what content to use and when as they are formulating their response.

The words and ideas of Art Costa (1991) epitomized the adopted philosophy of ILT about teaching methodology and thought. In his book *The School as a Home for the Mind*, Costa states:

> In a school that is a home for the mind there is an inherent faith that all people can continue to improve their intellectual capacities throughout life; that learning to think is as valid a goal for the at risk, handicapped, the disadvantaged, and the foreign-speaking as it is for the gifted and talented, and that all of us have the potential for even greater creativity and intellectual power. (p. 1)

Costa's words truly encompass the approach the team hoped that all teachers could take when entering any kind of classroom setting. The team found Costa's philosophy to be an optimistic one, encouraging the potential for learning in every person, regardless of limitations.

This is a philosophy ILT was able to promote. Homework assignments and projects would be designed so students use content to think. After being taught what a concept is and how it functions, students understand why they should learn something. Moreover they are challenged to create something new with the information learned. This is the approach to instruction the team utilized in the program.

THE THREADED MODEL LESSON DESIGN

The threaded model requires that thinking skills be threaded between the core classes, despite differences in subject matter. For the purposes of ILT, the chosen skills included prediction, inferences, deductive/inductive reasoning, contextual clues, fact/opinion, cause/effect, compare/contrast, classification, and sequencing. The lesson plans would include projects to foster critical thinking and require students to transfer knowledge, whether through note taking, an essay, pen and paper tests, or project-based assignments.

Fogarty (1991) described the threaded model as a meta-curricular approach that threads thinking skills, social skills, graphic organizers, study skills, and technology through various disciplines. ILT would successfully implement this meta-curricular approach, threading skills and teaching social skills through content for a well-rounded academic experience.

The skill-driven units would be taught for a minimum of two weeks. These skills would serve as the "hook" for retrieving information and therefore helped embed the information in the students' long-term memory, which helped improve the rate of retention. After each unit, each class would conduct an activity that applied the skill to the content. Later, each class would apply those skills in a "real-world" application that helped students better understand the significance of the skills outside the classroom.

The model itself proved less threatening to teachers who were hesitant about integrating content and possibly losing control of their courses. This model allowed control but forced integration with the skills common to the content. This threaded model would be used throughout the ILT process and at the end of each unit the skill would dictate the project design.

Benjamin Bloom and E. D. Hirsch (1987) criticized the fragmented approach of instruction that most educators used. For example, World War II would often be taught during its designated class time in social studies and the language arts class would be discussing *The Diary of Anne Frank*, yet neither teacher in the traditional classroom would help students make a deep connection between the novel and the war.

Conceptualizing the unit is just the first step; identifying the skills and their relevance to the content comes next. The team concluded that selecting the types of real-world experiences most appropriate for that skill and the content would be one of the most critical parts of lesson design.

It was a mission of ILT to eliminate this sort of fragmentation cited by Bloom and Hirsch through the threaded model. By addressing fragmentation in this manner, educators and students could better connect content to real-life applications by seeing how information might span two or more different subject areas. For example, the skill of prediction can be threaded in all subject areas. It can be used for estimation in math, forecasting current events in social studies, anticipating action in a novel in language arts, and hypothesizing in the science lab. By using this skill in all of their core class, students become cognizant of prediction, understanding when to use it, how to use it, and why.

Another example is student problem-solving skills in the area of conflict resolution. Language arts would allow students to resolve conflict between characters in the story. Social studies may accommodate resolving conflict between two countries. It is important to note that this threaded lesson would only work for the humanities but not for math and science. This is an example of what is meant by avoiding "force fit." Consequently, these courses would not be included in this lesson.

Heidi Hayes Jacobs (1989) cautioned educators about the notion of "force fit." In using this term, Jacobs was referencing the idea that there are times when the skill may not work for all courses, in which case it is possible to thread the skills between two or three classes but not four. It is important to recognize the consequences of force fitting because it often gives students misrepresentations about the content, which affects their understanding of the content.

Research like this, along with deliberate planning, would move the team closer to achieving its goal of making learning a priority and still promote the importance of critical thinking and thinking independently. The team was confident that the instructional plan developed for the program would yield successful results for the students.

The ILT team was determined to align academia and the students' perspective of their future as a way to motivate them to work toward their personal goals. Education institutions must make every effort to make these crucial connections through projects or service learning, both of which evolve from highly developed and well-planned curriculums and instruction.

The following examples illustrate how the threaded model was used. Please note that these are examples of the extended, skill-based threaded activity, which is part of a larger lesson plan. In ILT lesson plans, content was viewed as a means to an end, through which students could learn to connect content to the real world; it was not viewed as an end in itself or just to provide testing material.

Example 1

The team planned to incorporate the story "Chee's Daughter" into the ILT curriculum. The theme of this literary piece is how mankind's actions pollute the earth. Based on this theme, educators would thread skills of cause and effect and if/then throughout the courses.

These skills worked well in each content area. Language arts would focus on how progress pollutes the earth, discussing and analyzing other examples of causes and effects of pollution. In science, students would examine the effects of pollutants on the body and offer solutions for local pollutants. In math, students would analyze word problems around waste management, garbage, and recycling, while social studies classes would report on future conditions that would cause further pollution and identify ways pollution could be prevented.

The if/then skill was most effective in geometry problems. Continuing with the concept of pollution, students would be challenged to create an apparatus for disposing of garbage. To develop such an apparatus, students would be instructed to discuss the variance in material, size, and weight of the garbage using these considerations in the size and performance levels of the apparatus. As a culminating activity, the science class examined societal gains as a result of progress and the language arts class debated the science class on the topic: Progress Does or Does not Bring Growth.

The activities in each course had a centralized concept that allowed students to view that concept from multiple perspectives, namely, through the lens of their courses. For example, the emphasis on pollution and its effects on progress would permit students to develop shared understanding of subjects such as the Industrial Revolution and the concept of pollution in "Chee's Daughter."

Using content to examine real-world problems like pollution would not be just an academic discussion. In fact, the classes would be scheduled to engage in community service activities, including picking up garbage alongside tourist sites. These activities bridged school and community experiences. Additional activities to develop understanding of the content would include visits to government departments with interviews of the Department of Public Works personnel and writing reports.

Example 2

In another example, the language arts class would read an excerpt from John Steinbeck's 1939 novel, *The Grapes of Wrath*. The excerpt "The Flood" is about farmers heading west, seeking prosperity, and instead experiencing a cruel twist of fate: a flood. The overarching theme was the impact of nature on human lives.

This lesson seemed appropriate for a community that experienced hurricanes every year. As a result of the high winds from the hurricanes in the community, there was damage to buildings and public utilities, as well as flooding resulting from rising tides and excessive rain.

The students would be able to take the fundamental issues mentioned in the story and apply them to the reality of their own community. Utilizing the skills of compare and contrast, as well as persuasion, students engaged in activities that focused on natural disasters and the human condition.

In science classes, students assessed and cited potential health risks and recommended better post-disaster related health care services. Language arts classes would be expected to craft a letter requesting donations to restore a service that proved essential prior to the wake of the storm. Social studies compared and contrasted how early humans' ancestors and the farmers in the story dealt with natural disasters. Math students were asked to suggest ways land and shores could be protected from flooding and they also had to assess the adequacy of current standards for flood protection.

Example 3

In the story *Twelve Angry Men,* twelve jurors have heated debates as they attempt to come to consensus on a verdict. After reading the story, math students would be asked to come to a consensus with a classmate as to which geometry proof would be best to solve an assigned problem. Social studies students would have to choose "the best" civilization and persuade their readers why their choice was best. Science students would persuade "a doctor" to use a specified drug for a particular ailment. Language arts classes chose a position and defended it in a persuasive essay.

Example 4

In the short story "Contents of a Dead Man's Pocket," a man attempts to retrieve a piece of paper that blows onto the window sill in the days of typewriters. The man slips off the sill and plunges to his death while shoving the paper into his pocket.

Math classes would determine the rate at which someone would fall from varying heights. Social studies students would research occurrences of similar accidents and illustrate the frequency of these accidents using a graph. Language arts students would describe the scene of the accident, and those who wanted to pursue professional careers in law enforcement wrote police reports for the incident. The police report seemed like a particularly successful activity because it would resonate with students interested in pursuing careers in law enforcement.

Most of these extended assignments required students to write—an area that seemed to be the weakest for most students based on the previous school data. One of the interventions to address this problem entailed a baseline assessment to better understand what skills students needed to work on. ILT students would be asked to submit an essay to an outside company for assessment. The students would each pay $10 for the assessment.

Feedback on the essay would show results for ILT as a whole, each class, and each child. Copies of the assessment would be provided to parents as well. The assessments would rate students on mechanics and the overall structure of the essay. It would also outline for each student the areas of weakness to which immediate attention should be given.

Instruction would be customized for each student based on the feedback on their submitted work. At the end of the year, each student would submit another essay. The results would be used to track progress and assess student growth.

The learning activities in ILT would be designed to advance transfer of knowledge while cultivating thinking skills and promoting creativity and intuition. Students would be taught explicitly how to elaborate on their thoughts, and would be instructed on how to integrate, justify, and synthesize their ideas to reach a conclusion. These skills were intended to truly enrich student learning and these are skills that are required in the workplace as well.

Interpersonal skills could make or break the success of the program. In fact, at-risk students have been assessed as lacking such skills. Skills such as listening, using perspective-taking, talking in quiet voices, and were incapable of disagreeing without the use of racial slurs and derogatory terms. Interpersonal skills would be taught through instructional frameworks such as the Socratic seminar and cooperative learning techniques. The team developed a reflective tool to help students assess their behavior in groups. This tool would allow the groups to receive constructive feedback about their group processing skills.

While linking school to the student's outside world was important, learning activities had to include an element of fun. The work of David DeVries and Keith Edwards (1973) suggested the use of games to supplement course material. This process was also advocated by Robert Slavin (1974). Content for classroom games and competition varied based on what was covered in that unit. Games would only be incorporated in ILT if they served to improve student learning. ILT would use this medium as a way to engage students and encourage them to attend class and complete assignments.

A WORD ON ASSESSMENT

According to Borland (1986), students must know and understand the objectives of the assignment and the instructor must make the expectations clear before they begin a task. Assignment objectives include the requirements for a specific activity and the level of acceptable performance. The objective must be specific and measurable while connecting to a student's prior knowledge.

Educators in ILT ensured students understood all terms and relevant concepts. A student's level of understanding would be measured through activities, tests, and projects, as well as authentic and performance-based assessments. Grading has always been an issue of great debate in education. However, ILT utilized the same system of grading but the expectation was clearly outlined in a rubric. ILT defined content mastery as students understanding the content well enough that they could apply the content to create something "new." Students were able to chart their own progress in their notebooks.

ILT made clear distinctions between academic objectives and instructional objectives. Academic objectives indicated the percentage of improvement a group of students will acquire in a specified time. On the other hand, instructional objectives clearly state what students will be able to do at the end of the lesson. For example, by the end of a lesson, students will be able to use appropriate thinking skills to respond to questions.

Jacobs (1989) cited two additional areas to assess: the students' attitudinal change toward school and the impact of ILT. A program such as ILT would inevitably have some effect on student behavior. The impact of the program would be assessed against indicators that included attitudinal changes, attendance, writing, homework completion, final grades at the end of the year, and the level of parent involvement.

The ILT team did not have access to the at-risk students' previous year's records to capture attendance patterns and grades. Consequently, they were forced to make connections based on what previous knowledge they had. For example, a strong correlation seemed to exist between a student's poor performance and lack of motivation, high truancy rates, and poor time management skills, which translated into low homework completion rates and a failing grade. Surveys and interviews would be used to determine attitudinal changes in students.

INCENTIVES

Attempts to align students' educational experiences with their needs underscored the fact that success in academics means more than effective instruction. Simply put, if education does not consider the "whole child," success can be hampered. The team's definition of teaching for the "whole child" meant using content and the academic environment to foster learning and development of each child's individual's skills so he or she could be successful in the community.

The research concurs that one cannot teach in chaos. As an early step, the teachers would implement a set of rules and procedures (see appendix B) to maintain order in the classroom. The first weeks of school would be spent teaching the class rules and procedures as content. At-risk students have low levels of motivation. Quality teaching can lose its effectiveness if the learning environment is distorted as a result of student misbehavior, including unintentional behaviors that result from a lack of motivation.

Planning a research-based program to support student learning does not guarantee that it will be successful. Students must be motivated to fulfill the demands of the program. Therefore, a motivational program (appendix K) that provides incentives for students to complete their tasks would be implemented. In that system, ILT students would be given points for completing daily tasks. The system would also ensure that students come to class on time.

Traditionally, progress reports were sent home just before final report card distributions and did not afford any time for self-correction. Therefore, parents would receive ILT's progress report (appendix C) weekly, so students and parents could work together to improve academic weaknesses in "real time." The weekly reports would not be all bad news and reports would vary based on student accomplishments for the week.

The introduction of this additional report necessitated a change to policy; progress reports for ILT would be weekly not at the end of the semester as it was done in the district. This service was meant to assist students to improve in a timely and effective way. Requiring parents to review and sign the report would make them true partners since they would be aware of their child's classroom performance, behavior, and attendance.

In ILT, grades and attendance would matter. All students who made gains in the incentive rewards program and maintained a B average or higher would be acknowledged in the weekly ILT Newsletter. Through businesses' collaborating with ILT, and of course with parent consent, these students would be offered part-time jobs with a stipend during the Christmas and summer vacations as a reward for their academic achievements. The businesses in the program would also complete evaluations on each student working with them to assess the students' work ethics. ILT deliberately sought business partnerships with organizations that helped students improve their life skills.

Also, a tangible reward system would be in place for the one-year period that students would be in the ILT program. This would be another way to boost attendance: the extra credit points system (see appendix K). This system of rewards would be tied to academic achievement. One stipulation was that the student had to engage in the class activity. Today, a site exists with attendance tags to motivate students to attend school. These tags can be found at Imagestuff (www.imagestuff.com/programs/perfattend).

A class activity would be scheduled for each day of the week. For example, on Monday students would create a summary of a particular newspaper article that dealt with world affairs or current events related to the content currently being discussed in the class. The students could earn up to twenty-five points if the summary was accurate and if the news item was deemed newsworthy and appropriate for the content.

Attendance issues would be addressed through the Tuesday Early Bird Special (see appendix K). The first student to arrive to class on Tuesday would earn five points. On Wednesdays, the educator began the day with a question or two on content. Any students who answered correctly could earn up to thirty-five points.

On Thursday, the students would write in their weekly journals. They would select a topic from the curriculum and write a paragraph, adhering to all the rules of effective writing. Every student could earn up to fifty points on Thursday. On Friday, those who had perfect attendance for the week would be awarded five points. Students were motivated and, for the most part, participated fully in the incentive program. The team would also implement intangible rewards. Under this reward program, students would have the opportunity to earn community service points or present class work at the PTA meeting.

PARENTS AS PARTNERS

ILT was designed to be a true partnership of shared responsibility. The team would garner support from the parents by connecting them to available services that would help them to actively support their children. This partnership would go well beyond projects, bake sales, fundraising, and the distribution of report cards.

Parents would become copartners in ILT and as such become a pillar of support for the program. As suggested by the research, letters (appendix A) were sent to the parents introducing the program and the expectations, along with a note from the principal stating that parents could request that their child be moved out of the program. No such requests were made. All 483 students remained in the program.

Frequent communication about student progress would make parents a central part of the decision-making process in their children's education. Additionally, communication would not be just information sharing from educators. Two-way communication (Sasser, 1991; Clark, in Moles and D'Angelo, 1993) was most desirable because it meant that parents' voices would be heard. The information would be sent to ILT parents, with a balance of good and bad news, and would encourage parent involvement.

Communication with the parents had to be more interactive and supportive in ILT than in traditional programs. The weekly progress report implemented by ILT would give parents ongoing information, encouraging them to keep a close watch on their child's progress and, in so doing, motivate them to be a positive influence on their child's success. Even more important, they could assess their influence at the end of each week. Parents in the ILT program became true partners, and were instrumental in planning the child's post–high school experience along with the guidance department.

Parents would be made to feel trusted and valued partners in the academic process of their children, and a system would be developed to help parents support their children's educational endeavors with confidence. Education, school, and course content have evolved since parents went to school, so ILT would direct parents to the Saturday Academies where they could receive training in content and therefore be better able to support their children.

When dealing with parents, ILT would be aware of cultural sensitivities that may unintentionally challenge cultural beliefs. The manner in which institutions interact with parents influences the extent and quality of parental involvement with their children's learning. Prior to a PTA meeting for the school, the ILT teachers planned to hold meetings for its parents and at those meetings, students could showcase their work. Parent-teacher conferences would be conducted as a team rather than with one teacher. All the child's teachers in the team met with the parent.

These interactions were planned so that a sense of trust between parents and the ILT team would develop. ILT's goal was to build an atmosphere of trust, high expectations, fairness, generosity, and engender tolerance from parents. When necessary, educators would swap common planning time with lunch to accommodate parents' schedules. During the regular monthly PTA meetings, the team would arrange for baby-sitting services sponsored by the National Honor Society. These students provided the service to fulfill their community service requirements for graduation.

Both students and parents in ILT would benefit. Students who needed tutoring would have a request made to the Peer Leaders for their services. Peer Leaders were another student organization whose members were able to fulfill community service requirements by volunteering to tutor. This was an effective program because sometimes it was easier for students to understand the material when their peers were instructing. The ILT team would check the attendance rosters to determine if referred students were taking advantage of the services. Students who could not attend after school would be tutored at lunch time.

Parents are the school's first contact with the community. Some are business owners, other professionals, and others worked with businesses that networked with key individuals who could be beneficial to ILT's curriculum and career program. With this in mind, the team decided that it would catalog the careers listed by the students. As they got to know the parents, the team would identify those who could give presentations during the monthly Career Day activities (appendix J), and invite them as speakers.

In his work, Art Costa (1991) emphasized the importance of having knowledge beyond demographics about students to be served by any reform efforts. There were 483 students in the ILT program and the survey would be used to discover attributes of the students would matter for the program. For instance, attention to culture and embracing differences both supported and promoted a sense of belonging and a sense of communal-like family. Bilingual educators would be invited to parental conferences where they would function as translators. Parents who were not fluent in English would now feel welcome and be invited to contribute to their child's academic success. The educators' goal was to create strong partnerships with their students' parents. Parent support and interest could be measured by attendance to functions and their level of commitment to plan their child's post–high school experience.

SUPPORTING ILT THROUGH PARTNERSHIPS

Partnerships promote the sustenance of any program; ILT would be no different. As noted, ILT planned to establish partnerships with local businesses to offer achieving students part-time jobs during Christmas and summer. Collaboration with the business community was vital in the development of the career program, which would keep the students focused on their goal. Done well, this would enhance the goals of ILT. In an effort to deal with the "whole child," ILT would collaborate with the Vision Center to provide free eye exams for the students.

In terms of partnering with other education entities, the guidance department would be instrumental in providing support to ILT through classroom visits to offer and explain guidance services. The department also granted permission for the tenth graders in ILT to attend the college fairs normally reserved for upperclassmen. In addition, the team would engage with local agencies such as the Youth Multi-Service Center (see appendix J), which offered preemployment attitudinal skills training. This training helped emphasize dropout prevention. The Youth Multi-Service Center also offered counseling for real-life experiences. Their services supported the social and nonacademic aspects of the program.

Partnerships went beyond the district. Outside consultants such as the Bay Area Writing Project, Robin Fogarty, and the researcher/teacher from California who designed Paper Geometry, would be invited to conduct professional development sessions, since their work would support the ILT program. These consultants would strengthen the academic skills of the team members in writing, geometry, and even the development of integrated lesson planning.

ILT also partnered with the school monitors whose assistance would provide the students with experiences aimed at making them re-think their behavior and attitudes. The monitors would invite the students with extreme behavioral issues to the Scared Straight program. In this program, students visited the prisons where inmates discussed their mistakes and regrets. For most students, this was an eye-opener. This experience clearly detailed the quality of the life they could expect if they continued down the paths of destructive and reckless behavior. These experiences at the Scared Straight program, in conjunction with monthly school assemblies, aimed to improve student behavior and modify their social skills.

Gang-related activities were monitored and addressed through the cooperative efforts of the police department who assigned a police officer to monitor gang violence at the school. The ILT team would collaborate with the police officer who was also connected to psychologists. The police officer connected ILT with psychologists who worked with the students in groups as well as individually. When necessary, the guidance department would identify community resources to help parents care for their children. The police officer also showed deep concern for these students on a personal level. Several students admired his friendly nature and he became a real role model for students wishing to pursue professional careers in law enforcement.

One of the key components of the program was the support from the school's principal and the local teachers' union. Both district and union support were necessary. Before the adjustments in location and schedule for ILT teachers could be finalized, approval had to be gotten from those two entities. It was clear that addressing student learning, students' family, and truancy were compelling enough to garner the support and approval of the principal and the local union.

But approval is only the first step. To be successful, programs like ILT require will, determination, and a vision for the future. Funding will never be sufficient and education is always being challenged to do more with less. However, those in charge of grooming and preparing the next generation of professionals will now know that a lack of funding is a poor excuse for not attempting to educate students in an effective way. Work with supporters such as parents, your biggest allies, the principal, teacher leaders, mentors, and the community to support student learning. It is now everybody's responsibility.

As the program—geared at supporting at-risk students—advanced, the team understood that developers must be deliberate about the changes necessary to adequately accommodate new programs in the school. Creative approaches had been taken to address the scheduling needs of ILT and the sequencing of ILT courses, which allowed teahceres to trade and combine time. The resulting double periods would allow students more time for methodical and in-depth processing for difficult and complex course materials. It was this type of adaptability and flexibility that enhanced student engagement.

ACADEMIC, CAREER, AND LIFE SKILLS

The life skills program was designed to give these adolescents a glimpse at adult responsibilities. As part of the career program, designated class periods were dedicated to teaching ILT students simple life skills. For example, the ability to read and follow instructions when filling out application forms was another important component of the career program. Students would learn how to fill out the Small Business Application (SBA) form. The same went for drivers' education and drivers' license forms, passport applications, and income tax return forms.

The students who got the part-time jobs would learn to keep financial logs. These students, using a simulation of a checkbook, would enter their paycheck amounts and record their expenditures and balances. Another motivator and business experience activity was raising funds for the prom. This class would be sponsors of the prom next year in the eleventh grade, and the ILT team used fundraising as a learning activity. The students became more proficient in planning and bookkeeping. For example, they had to assess the souvenirs and the decorations and decide how much money they had to raise.

All of this was done without considering prom dues. Their creativity was put to the test since they had to develop various fund-raisers that did not take too much money, if any, to set up. These activities also evoked a sense of community and belonging for the students and helped them develop much-needed social skills.

The best-laid plans can end up in disarray if certain extraneous factors are not addressed. For instance, all the planning done by the team would not produce the expected results if the focus was solely on academic achievement.

For example, at-risk students typically have poor time-management skills. Other students may have the same poor skills but it does not seem to affect them as much. To help students learn to manage time, Bullock and Gall (1990) recommends that students be provided timelines and rubrics for projects. Additionally, they suggest students be taught how to organize binders, how to use assignment sheets effectively, be given an overview to understand the school schedule, and be told what the rules and procedures are.

In addition, Barry Zimmerman (1986) suggests that students be given a study schedule so they are deterred from studying the night before the test. Providing students with a study schedule would support effective and productive time management. For the students who need a more structured learning environment, the timeline would include dates for specific parts of the project or task. ILT would incorporate these strategies in the program.

The team also understood that most homes had a television and video games but lacked "print rich" materials. Therefore, the library and a librarian would play a central role in ILT.

A librarian would be assigned to work with the team. The role here would be a little different. In addition to the introductory session to the library, the librarian and the library would be an integral part of lesson design. When the skills were identified and the project designed, the team would inquire of the librarian about the types of resources that were available for the students to use. The librarian would make a list of the resources as a reference to provide assistance when students could not locate a resource on the topic they were working on. The use of the library was another critical skill in the ILT program.

Social skills were also extremely important to the proper implementation of cooperative learning. Without adequate social skills, students may have difficulty becoming proficient in the lessons that were taught in group settings. In addition, important skills such as those outlined by the SCANS Report might be missed. The ILT team hoped that cooperative learning, combined with the lesson framework of the threaded model, plus extended projects would help students attain the necessary social skills for learning and for life.

Resources such as *Blueprints for Thinking in the Cooperative Classroom* by James Bellanca and Robin Fogarty (1991) provided guidelines for building social skills. David Johnson and Roger Johnson (1984) also emphasized the capability of cooperative learning to promote socialization. The extent to which schools can contribute to a student's psychological well-being, offer accommodations that strengthen those qualities, and nurture those predispositions of cooperative learning, which result in a well-mannered individual, cannot be overemphasized.

Johnson and Johnson outlined the steps for the successful implementation of cooperative learning. These steps include addressing such elements as speaking in six-inch voices, listening to each other, staying with the group, doing the job, and helping each other.

The researchers warned that students sitting around a table did not constitute a research-based implementation of cooperative learning. To foster the efficient working of groups, the team planned to challenge classes to complete tasks and work effectively with each other. Classroom activities promoted group work, positive interdependence, and social skills. Cooperative social skills were central to student success.

Despite the use of cooperative learning, the ILT curriculum was not going to be one-size-fits-all, nor would its structure allow students of high ability to just slide through. Johnson and Johnson (1984) in the book *Circles of Learning: Cooperation in the Classroom* recommended this type of instruction since it prepares students to be functioning social beings in the real world of work. The skills learned in a cooperative learning setting are indeed an asset to how one can function in society and amass the skills cited in the SCANS Report. All students can benefit from this type of instruction.

There is great benefit in becoming proficient in the subset of skills that support cooperative learning activities. Such skills include communication, "perspective taking," and listening to each other. Added to the curriculum were the skills of summarizing, paraphrasing, and note taking. Having students become proficient in these skills was an essential goal of the program.

The Socratic method also served as the instructional framework to enhance the social skills of listening, the art of discussion, and to promote tolerance—fundamental in the ILT program. In such a setting the team hoped to strengthen the students' ability to sense tone, disagree with ideas and not the individual, keep an open mind to see all points of view, and contribute ideas.

A common frustration of at-risk students is their inability to articulate their thoughts. As a result, ILT decided that it would be important to teach the students to express themselves clearly, to seek clarity through paraphrasing and summarizing, and, when faced with a problem, to be able to probe to understand, generate alternative solutions, and seek consensus. Having mastered these skills, the student would be equipped to work in a team, hopefully make decisions and solve problems. Some of the skills were cited in the SCANS Report. As such, students would sense increased efficacy in intra- and interpersonal skills.

PROGRAM CHALLENGES

Several existing policies could have hindered ILT if the school administration had not been open to adjusting them. This school's practice of assigning homework each night was contrary to research, which advocated that homework should be assigned only when students truly understand the content. In fact, the role of homework in ILT was to have students practice information already learned to reinforce classroom teachings and to challenge students to create something new with the content learned. The research information then influenced the rethinking of the homework policy for ILT. It was no longer mandatory for ILT to assign homework every night and the team was able to create assignments that required the students to apply their new knowledge to real-world events.

Obstacles to a program's success are sometimes belief systems rather than policies. Several aspects of ILT had either expanded or flatly rejected policies and actions that did not support student learning. More important was that four teachers and a facilitator were able to make these changes a reality. The challenge would come when the team and the principal would attempt to get the "buy in" from the rest of the faculty. ILT was established for a good cause, student safety and learning, but would the rest of the faculty see it that way?

The principal's concern that the school's own faculty could derail a good suggestion was very real. Some of the staff members' negative reactions to the program should come as no surprise but were still astonishing. Instead of asking about the goals of the program and how the team intended to obtain the goals, the faculty did not think ILT was going to work. No one even asked about the assessment mechanism that would be used to determine the program's success.

The setting here is the first faculty meeting at the beginning of the school year. The criticisms (in italics), are followed by an abbreviated record of what the principal said. They are listed here so that those faced with a similar experience will be able to respond if such criticism is offered.

1. To preserve school safety and closely monitor attendance, a special wing will be devoted to the program.

    Dedicating an entire wing of the school to the ILT program was considered a privilege for favorites.

    The principal responded by quoting statistics about fights and other incidences that required a police presence. In addition, the academic data was also mentioned. He explained that conditions, as simple as classroom arrangements, can lead to loss of instructional time and hinder academic progress. Such loss was avoided here because the ILT program was able to utilize classrooms that were adjacent to each other. Teachers could arrange the classes to support instruction without having to take valuable time to rearrange the class to its original setup for the next instructor.

2. For the program to succeed, reduced ILT-teacher workload was necessary. However, their class sizes could be as many as thirty-two.

    A lighter workload means more students in our classes and yet we all get the same pay.

    The principal stated that the class sizes may be bigger and asked if there would be volunteers to form another team. When he clarified that there would be no extra pay to do this, there were no volunteers.

3. The program would be evaluated by identified indicators. It would not just be grades.

    Will the students in the ILT team take the same departmental test?

    The principal assured the faculty that the students in ILT would take the same departmental exam.

4. This school-within-a-school structure also meant that some teachers were functioning as quasi-administrators.

    That's against the contract. They just want to be administrators.

    The principal pointed out that he had faith in his faculty and did not feel the need to micromanage the program. He had many more things to attend to. He assured the faculty that he would be on top of the program.

5. To accomplish the tasks necessary to support the program, the ILT teachers would use the last period of the day for planning, meetings, and professional development.

    The faculty argued that the team already had a contractual planning time and besides, the local union, also an affiliate of national AFT, had a professional development program.

    The principal introduced the concept of job-embedded. Two things: these teachers should not be asked to put in more personal time for the program and the topics on the local professional development calendar were not what the team was looking for at the

moment. The principal did state that the local program was a
strong research-based program.

Despite the criticism, the principal was able to convince the staff that
raising student achievement, stemming the rising dropout rates, and improving school safety were important aspects of the program. In the end,
ILT received provisional support: if success was not evident by the end of
the school year, it was gone.

Effective programs use existing data to amend program structure and
services. Obtaining significant data on time was a challenge to the ILT
program. The data from the current year's standardized test would not
be released to the school until two to three months into the following
school year—too late to implement any meaningful corrective plans. The
team requested the assistance of the principal to work with the research
department so that the scores for the standardized tests were released
before school closed for the summer.

FUNDING

Projects cannot survive without some type of funding, no matter how
limited. Funding is essential for the procurement of materials, staffing,
activities, and further training in specialized areas. Since the integrated
curriculum is different from what exists in traditional schools there were
distinctly different needs for additional training and materials.

ILT received $10,000 from Title I funding from the principal and a
grant funded by the National Endowment for the Humanities produced
another $10,000. The grant money was received in November of the
school year. Operating costs (appendix M) were minimal and most of the
funding would be used for professional development and to cover the
price for the second student essay assessment.

SUMMARY

The ILT teachers were willing to be creative and function "out of the
box." The Early Bird program for attendance, the adjacent classrooms,
the career program, and established partnerships were all implemented
in a unique and systematic way. Team members were amenable to closely monitoring student learning, producing more frequent progress reports on academic and behavior achievements, and becoming part of a
learning community. With regards to instruction, skills were taught using content and extended assignments fostered real-world applications.

It was the hope of the team members that such systematic changes would permit students served by ILT to receive the type of education that could ensure the acquisition of the following:

- proficiency in communication, whether through writing or speech
- the ability to think critically, problem solve, and work in a team
- the ability to transfer skills and knowledge to new situations
- a greater knowledge of career options and plans
- an increased yearly proficiency in the four core subject areas by 3 percent

ILT was a research-based program that set out to address the issue of safety. However, if all that changed was having the classes physically and academically close to each other, the effect of the program might have been limited. In the end, more than that changed and it became apparent to the teachers in ILT that creating a dynamic, interactive learning environment that fosters academic success in a nurturing, communal, and constructive way is crucial in improving education.

FOUR

The Impact of ILT

ILT was developed to preserve school safety and support student learning. Ideally, the team would have had a year to plan; however, a situation that appears to threaten learning and safety calls for immediate, coherent action. The urgency of the matter did not relieve ILT from the guidelines for other programs. There were defined expectations followed by an assessment of success indicators to determine its levels of impact.

The indicators used to assess the impact of ILT included attendance records, homework completion rates, feedback from the writing assessment company, changes in attitude toward school and family, changes in parent and community involvement, and the end-of-the-school-year grades. ILT was not intended to be a scientific study, but it was expected to show results through a district mandate.

Income restrictions to attend this public school placed all the tenth-grade students in similar socioeconomic categories, making them an acceptable sample. Two groups within this sample, the students enrolled in ILT and those who were not, would be compared to determine the effectiveness of the program. The characteristics of ILT—for example, its proven research base, instructional processes, and academic supports—made it significantly different from the rest of the tenth grade. This made comparing the results between the two groups acceptable.

For example, all tenth graders attended the career assemblies. That was the principal's decision. All students would write an essay on the assembly but only ILT students made the assemblies an integral part of post–high school planning.

To conduct a comparative analysis of the grades at the end of the year, a baseline score had to be established. All students in the tenth grade would take the departmental exams. A baseline score or performance level could only be established for language arts and writing. The curriculum in both ninth and tenth grades for language arts focused on the same thing—genres of literature with a writing component. The content of the other courses had changed. Therefore, ILT would focus on passing rates for the present school year. The team did, however, request from the students a copy of their ninth-grade-year report card.

The team hoped that the report card would give an overview of the students' disposition to learning and overall performance. A comparison of these scores indicated that the average grade in language arts in the previous year was 72 percent and by the end of the new school year it was 89 percent. The sixteen students also performed well; average grades for language arts rose from 60 percent to 80 percent. In writing, a baseline was set using the services of a writing assessment company.

The students would submit an essay defending a career choice. Based on the multiple forms of feedback on the essay from the company, ILT would develop its writing program. A careful perusal of the feedback from the company about individual students allowed ILT's writing program to have an individual component. Students worked on their individual areas of weakness. Reports of the assessment were given to the teacher, and both students and their parents received the individual student's results. Students paid $10 to the company for the pre-assessment of their writing.

The process was repeated at the end of the year; the end-of-year feedback was compared to the initial feedback. Details were cumbersome, but overall, the students' writing improved individually and as a class. Student performance in both language arts and writing would be used as measures of success.

Departmental exams were administered to all tenth graders at the end of the year. Final grades provided a valid means to assess ILT's impact on student learning. Course comparisons between the years were difficult since, except for language arts, the students were enrolled in new courses. Math was now geometry, science was now biology, and social studies was now world history. Therefore, success would be assessed using the passing rates for each course in ILT compared to the other tenth graders. ILT would also assess the extent to which nonacademic indicators such as behavior, attitude, and parent involvement changed.

Although this program was not conducted as a scientific study, a strong correlation can be made between the instructional processes used in ILT and the achievement levels of the students in the program.

ILT had 483 students in the program, assigned to four teachers, each of whom had four classes. The registrar tried to have all 483 students registered in ILT, but gross overcrowding left some students with fewer than four classes within the team, and sometimes only one. The team worked with this constraint and disaggregated the data on student achievement by the number of ILT classes taken by the students.

Students who had four classes in ILT were designated as "pure" and students having fewer than four classes were designated as "un-pure." To assess levels of student achievement, the school's grade printout of final grades for the year was used. The team disaggregated the data in the following ways:

- Passing rate of students who had four classes with ILT
- Passing rate of students who had three classes with ILT
- Passing rate of students who had two classes with ILT
- Passing rate of students who had one class with ILT

Of the 483 students served by ILT, 72.05 percent (348) were pure; these had four classes with ILT. Therefore, 27.95 percent (135) were un-pure, meaning they had fewer than the four classes in ILT. An examination of the grade printout for the 348 pure ILT students indicated that in math, 84 percent (293) passed and 16 percent (55) failed. In language arts, 82 percent (284) passed and 18 percent (64) failed. Eighty-one percent (281) passed and 19 percent (67) failed in social studies, and in science, 65 percent (225) passed and 35 percent (123) failed (see table 4.1).

Table 4.1.   Passing Rates for Pure Students (Four ILT Classes) (n = 348)

Subjects	Pass	Fail
Math	84% (293)	16% (55)
Language Arts	82% (284)	18% (64)
Social Studies	81%(281)	19% (67)
Science	65% (225)	35% (123)

Source: High School End of Year Grade Printout SY 91–92

An examination of the schedules of the un-pure students showed an enrollment distribution of 61 un-pure students in three ILT classes, forty-three in two, and thirty-one in one. The sixty-one students were enrolled in language arts, social studies, and math. The forty-three students were in only social studies and math. The thirty-one were enrolled in only science. The enrollment distribution appears in table 4.2.

Table 4.2.   Distribution of Un-Pure Students Enrolled in ILT (n=135)

3 Classes	2 Classes	One Class
45% (61)	32% (43)	23% (31)

Source: High School End of Year Grade Printout SY 91–92

The performances of the 135 un-pure students in ILT were also assessed. Of the sixty-one un-pure students who had three ILT classes (language arts, social studies, math), 77 percent (47) passed all three, 13 percent (8) passed two (social studies, math), 7 percent (4) passed one (social studies), and 3 percent (2) failed all three classes.

Of the forty-three students enrolled in social studies and math, 53 percent (23) passed the two classes, 21 percent (9) passed just math, and 26 percent (11) failed both classes. The thirty-one students who had only one ILT class (science) had a 58 percent (18) passing rate, while 42 percent (13) failed that course (see table 4.3).

Table 4.3.   Passing Rates of Un-Pure ILT Students (students with fewer than four classes) (n = 135)

Number of Classes	Pass Three Classes	Pass Two Classes	Pass One Class (Sc)	Failed
Three (n=61) (LA, SS, M)	77% (47) (LA, SS, M)	13% (8) (SS, M)	6% (4) (SS)	3% (2)
Two (n=43) (SS, M)	—	53% (23) (SS, M)	21% (9) (M)	26% (11)
One (n=31) (Sc)	—	—	58% (18) (Sc)	42% (13)

Source: High School End of Year Grade Printout SY 91–92

ILT was positively affecting student learning. Those results underscored a strong correlation between the frequency of exposure to the instructional designs and support structures in ILT and the rate of passing. The team proceeded to disaggregate the grade distribution data of the un-pure students by course, based on number of ILT classes.

Of the sixty-one students enrolled in three ILT classes—language arts, social studies, and math—77 percent (47) passed all three. The distribution reveals that even the un-pure students in three ILT classes were performing between the A and B range for the most part. Table 4.4 captures the grade distribution.

Table 4.4.   Grade Distribution for Un-Pure Students Passing All Three ILT Classes (n = 47)

	Language Arts	Social Studies	Math
A (100-90)	65% (31)	72% (34)	31% (15)
B (89-80)	23% (11)	17% (8)	48% (23)
C (79-70)	10% (5)	10% (5)	14% (7)
F (69)			

Source: High School End of Year Grade Printout SY 91–92

In addition, eight of the sixty-one students passed two of the three courses: social studies and math. Once again, the achievement rates fall between As and Bs. Table 4.5 captures the grade distribution.

Table 4.5.   Grade Distribution for Un-Pure Students Passing Two Out of Three ILT Classes (n = 8)

	Language Arts	Social Studies	Math
A (100—90)		37% (3)	25% (2)
B (89—80)		37% (3)	50% (4)
C (79—70)		25% (2)	25% (2)
F (69—)			

Source: High School End of Year Grade Printout SY 91–92

Four students (6 percent) of the sixty-one enrolled in three ILT classes passed one class: science. In science, 25 percent (1) of the students had an A, 25 percent (1) had a B, and 50 percent (2) had a C. Two students (3 percent) failed all three classes (see table 4.6).

Table 4.6.   Grade Distribution for Un-Pure Students Passing One Out of Three ILT Classes (n=4)

	Science	Social Studies	Math
A (100–90)	25% (1)		
B (89–80)	25% (1)		
C (79–70)	50% (2)		
F (69)			

Source: High School End of Year Grade Printout SY 91–92

The students who had fewer than four courses in ILT still did remarkably well, but as highlighted in the tables, the number of As and Bs were reduced as students had fewer classes with ILT. These results appeared to support the idea that increased exposure to the instructional methods, pedagogy, and structures of ILT supported student achievement.

Table 4.7.   Grade Distribution for Un-Pure Students Enrolled in Two ILT Classes and Passing Both (n = 23)

	Language Arts	Social Studies	Math
A (100–90)		27% (12)	27% (12)
B (89–80)		20% (9)	18% (8)
C (79–70)		4% (2)	6% (3)
Fail (69)			

Source: High School End of Year Grade Printout SY 91–92

Forty-three students in ILT were enrolled in two classes (language arts and math). Twenty-three students passed two classes. Twelve students

(27 percent) received As in social studies and math, nine (20 percent) received Bs in social studies, and eight (18 percent) received Bs in math. Two (4 percent) received Cs in social studies and three (6 percent) received Cs in math. The grade distributions for that group are illustrated in table 4.7.

Of the forty-three students enrolled in two ILT classes, nine (21 percent) students passed one class. Five students passed social studies and four passed math. The grade distribution for these students is illustrated in table 4.8.

Table 4.8. Grade Distribution by Course for Un-Pure Students Enrolled in Two ILT Classes and Passing One Class (n = 9)

	Language Arts	Social Studies	Math
A (100–90)		22% (2)	11% (1)
B (89–80)		22% (2)	22% (2)
C (79–70)		11% (1)	11% (1)
Fail (69)			

Source: High School End of Year Grade Printout SY 91–92

Thirty-one of the 135 un-pure students were enrolled in one ILT class: science. Despite limited exposure to the instruction by the team, eighteen students passed that class. The grade distribution for these students is reflected in table 4.9.

Table 4.9. Grade Distribution by Course for Un-Pure Students Enrolled in One ILT Class and Passing (n = 18)

	Science	Language Arts	Social Studies	Math
A (100–90)	29% (9)			
B (89–80)	16% (5)			
C (79–70)	12% (4)			
Fail (69)				

Source: High School End of Year Grade Printout SY 91–92

Again, these results suggested that there were benefits from the type of activities and instruction the team performed in ILT. The purpose of the grade distribution was to get a snapshot of the progress made by students in ILT compared to the snapshot given by the previous year's report card. Grade distributions would not be done for the school, just the passing rates for each course. The district did not request that level of comparison.

The team, however, wanted to have an idea of the progress of the other tenth graders, referred to here as "the school." The school (the rest of the tenth grade) had an enrollment of 528 students who were shared by four teachers but not in the same structure as ILT. This distribution was based on departmental scheduling. Students were not blocked or annexed to each other in classes and, unless a student was disagreeable and noncompliant, teachers might choose to talk to parents but not to each other.

The results for the school were examined in a manner similar to ILT:

- Passing rate of students who had four classes with the school
- Passing rate of students who had three classes with the school
- Passing rate of students who had two classes with the school
- Passing rate of students who had one class with the school

Similar to ILT, students had a range of four, three, two, or even one class with the school. Therefore, a comparative assessment was made for passing rates between students who had all four classes in the school and ILT.

Of the 528 students in the school, 393 had all four core classes with the school and 135 students were shared between ILT and school due to scheduling challenges. Of the 393 students who had all four classes in the school, 59 percent (230) passed language arts and 41 percent (163) failed. In math, 47 percent (183) passed and 53 percent (210) failed. In social studies, 46 percent (179) passed and 54 percent (214) failed. In science, 52 percent (205) passed and 48 percent (188) failed. Table 4.10 represents these findings.

Table 4.10. Passing Rates for Students with All Four Classes with the School (n = 393)

Subjects	Pass	Fail
Language Arts	59% (230)	41% (163)
Math	47% (183)	53% (210)
Social studies	46% (179)	54% (214)
Science	52% (205)	48% (188)

Source: High School End of Year Grade Printout SY 91–92

Comparisons of the passing rates indicate that ILT had accomplished the goal of making at-risk students succeed. In math, ILT had an 84 percent passing rate, while the school had a 47 percent passing rate. Language arts students in ILT had an 82 percent passing rate, compared to 59 percent for the school. In social studies, ILT's passing rate was 81 percent and the school's was 46 percent. In science, ILT students had a 65 percent passing rate, compared to 52 percent in the school.

The team also examined the performance of the 135 students who were shared between ILT and the school. In the school, sixty-one of the 135 students in the school were enrolled in science only—they had the three other classes with ILT. Seventy percent (43) passed and 30 percent (18) failed science. One could surmise that the strategies taught in the ILT did have an effect on how well the students did.

Skills had been taught to a level of automaticity that allowed for an easy transfer of those skills. Only a correlation could be made but it seemed safe to say that teaching study habits, time management, and learning strategies that fostered reflection on one's meta-cognition would have an impact.

Forty-three students of the shared 135 un-pure students were enrolled in two courses (science and language arts) with the school. Of those forty-three students, 37 percent (16) passed and 63 percent (27) failed science. In language arts, 58 percent (25) passed and 42 percent (18) failed. In addition, 31 students had three courses in the school. In language arts, 68 percent (21) passed and 32 percent (10) failed. In math, 55 percent (17) passed and 45 percent (14) failed. In social studies, 81 percent (25) passed and 19 percent (6) failed.

The results spoke volumes. According to the passing rates, ILT students performed better than students in the school. This was not a scientific study, but a comparison of the passing rates between ILT and the school would fulfill the district mandate since the students took the same exam. Students in ILT seemed to have a deep understanding of the course content and skills in a way that allowed them to apply knowledge in new settings. This was evidenced by the fact that of the thirty-one students who had just one ILT course, 58 percent of those students passed that class.

The social studies results for the thirty-one students who had three classes with the school provoked an examination of classroom interactions. Eighty-one percent (25) of the students passed. This was a class that was taking social studies for the second time. A brief visit to that class revealed that the social studies teacher made sure her students knew the reason for studying the unit. They also understood how the units connected. Many activities in her class called for speeches and debates on topics in the content. This was an unusual approach for teachers in the traditional school where tests functioned as the only means of assessment. In fact, if too many students passed a test, it was deemed too easy and if many failed, the teacher was deemed unsatisfactory.

This teacher incorporated project-based instructional designs so the students would not be bored. Project-based learning made the class stimulating but the confines of the educational environment in which she operated may not have allowed her to do more. No one wants a renegade in the system but professionals should be given the opportunity to try.

Overall, ILT had a higher passing rate than the school. The team recognized that their result was not that of a scientific study but an assessment of ILT grade distribution demonstrated a correlation between ILT and student achievement. And certainly, the team considered whether students were getting assistance outside of ILT or school. However, several components of ILT were nonexistent in the school, which made the ILT results even more significant. Obviously, certain teaching methods yield results, as the social studies teacher demonstrated in her class.

The school-within-a-school framework created a positive learning environment for at-risk students; schoolwork was connected to life experiences. The threaded model of instructional design provided an opportunity to create connections within and between course content with real-world applications. Addressing academic and social needs through the use of a cooperative learning setting was unique to ILT. These are just a few of the attributes of ILT that made it different from the school.

Unlike the school, which relied on the school handbook and communications when infractions like nonattendance occurred, ILT utilized several methods to address the attendance issue. Explicit communication made expectations clear to parents and students; attendance was expected. Incentives for daily attendance such as an extra credit program (appendix K), support for homework completion, and adjacent classrooms motivated students to attend school and complete homework, and therefore reduced incidences of class cutting.

Success in academics was not the only goal of ILT. Attendance was also a goal and by the second month, student absenteeism in ILT dropped from an average of eight to ten absences in the first month to four to five absences in the second month. By the end of the school year, a few students still had unacceptable attendance rates but overall, absenteeism was due to sickness, unexpected family travel, or a planned visit to a business such as the Social Security Office, at which the student's presence was required. Reports on attendance in the school population indicated that absenteeism rates were much higher.

It was evident at the end of the year that the students with high rates of absenteeism had two or fewer classes in ILT. Of the forty-three un-pure students enrolled in two ILT classes, 63 percent (27) had acceptable attendance patterns and 37 percent (16) had unacceptable rates of more than four unexcused absences within a month. Of the thirty-one un-pure students who had one class with ILT, 65 percent (20) had acceptable attendance and 35 percent (11) had unacceptable attendance patterns. Students who had three classes with ILT had 87 percent (53) acceptable rates of attendance while 13 percent (8) had unacceptable rates.

In comparison to ILT's 348 pure students who had all four classes with the team, 83 percent (248) had acceptable rates of attendance and 16 percent (59) had unacceptable rates. According to attendance records, attendance rates proved satisfactory in the other classes attended by students with four to three classes in ILT. An acceptable rate was considered having fewer than two absences for a month, in which case excuses were provided and approved.

The library played a pivotal role in lesson design and in the homework process. According to the library's records, after implementation of ILT, circulation increased from 253 to 360 books in the first two months and to 2,415 by the end of the year. The library became a center for learning, as students in ILT were given assignments that required extensive use of the library. The librarians collaborated with team members prior to the issuance of assignments. This was one way to combat the lack of a "print-rich" environment. Normally students would have a library orientation and be left on their own to befriend the library. Occasionally a report would be assigned that would force the student to use the library.

As a result of this type of support, the completion rates of assignments and homework increased substantially. ILT students wrote numerous research papers and the quality of the papers improved tremendously by the end of the year. Success could be attributed to the preparation, making resources available and known, and the incentives available to students for completing their assignments.

No baseline was established for homework completion but a review of attendance books indicates that it had been a problem over the years. The assignments, extended projects, and extra credit incentives motivated students to complete their homework, which consequently fostered a deeper understanding of the content. Homework completion rates for the 483 students revealed that 88 percent of the students in ILT completed homework assignments. The fewer classes students had with ILT, the lower their rate of completion.

ILT's goals were set on the "whole child"; therefore, its successes cannot focus on academics alone. These students also learned how to be social. Social skills were practiced and taught at events such as picnics, movie night, and school shows. Assemblies set the groundwork and by the time they were employed in a part-time job, they understood the importance of having the skills stated in SCANS. The evaluation that employers were given to assess the students were on some of the skills outlined by SCANS. The evaluations indicate that the students who qualified for the jobs had those skills.

Students in ILT also learned life skills. Students who worked practiced balancing a checkbook. In their ILT classes, they learned to fill out forms such as tax forms, driver's license applications, and even applications for Small Business Administration loans. As much of the students' work as possible was done in a collaborative, cooperative learning setting, which the teachers participated in as well. The work ethics that students practiced in the classroom extended to the workplace, as noted by the employers.

Innovative programs such as ILT could not be as successful without the support of parents. Not only did ILT create a partnership with the parents and students, it also offered opportunities for parents to feel more effective at helping their children. Saturday Academies provided opportunities for parents to learn how to best help their children succeed.

Parents were not the only partners. Members of the business community offered services, jobs, free vision exams, and gave their time to present at assemblies. The in-school partners were involved as well. For example, the nurse made the students aware of nutrition. The guidance department assisted with post–high school plans and connected parents to appropriate services. The school monitors and cafeteria workers contributed to the students' social training.

By the year's end, the students were not the only ones who had experienced change. For the teachers, this had been a journey of change around beliefs, roles, and practices. In ILT, the teacher was a learner too and changed enough to allow other teachers into their classes to observe and give feedback. Several professional development hours, whether presented by a teacher or by a visiting consultant, supported the personal and professional growth of all parties.

One of the teachers put it this way:

> Lesson planning transformed from just an exercise to fulfill district mandates, to a vehicle for examining student performance and making modifications. ILT helped us get away from the textbook-driven curriculum to using the curriculum to develop lessons that prepared students for life making sure they have mastered content and employability skills. (J. C., educator in ILT, interviewed June 1991)

SUMMARY

Many factors contributed to ILT's success. The program addressed the needs of the whole child. Attendance problems were addressed through academic incentives and the lack of motivation was curtailed by connecting career choices to what was achieved in school. Instruction facilitated connections between courses and real-life experiences. Through the experience of a part-time job, students learned to balance a checkbook and fill out everyday forms such as driver license and passport applications. This coherent approach to supporting student learning yielded success beyond the projected 3 percent increase in academic achievement.

What the data showed was that components of ILT had a profound effect on student learning. Students who had all four core classes in ILT did extremely well. But even as scheduling hardships forced some students to be enrolled in only one class with ILT, they still did better than the students who had no classes with ILT.

The ultimate goal of ILT was not simply academic achievement; it was to find a way to use reform to support the whole child. To do that, other facets of the program had to be considered to support nonacademic factors that, if not addressed, would derail or diminish the impact of ILT.

Reform should not just be about scores or grades but should seek to support student learning in a way that helps them actualize their dreams.

On July 29, 2011, *Education Week* blogger Diette Courrege reported on the success of two rural schools, highlighted at an American Youth Policy Forum. The blog entry, titled "How Two Rural Schools Prepare Kids for College Part 1," reports that these schools had a 100 percent graduation rate. One of the schools afforded students the opportunity for dual credits. In doing so, students, in addition to the high-school diploma, were able to earn up to thirty graduate credits.

One of the main focuses of these schools was on at-risk students and college transition. The blog did not go into detail as to what programs or supports were given to the students. But based on what we now know, the students must have found themselves in a highly challenging school environment that made certain students understand the importance of an education.

The Integrated Learning Team had a vision that supported student learning and included similar and additional components, perhaps not implemented the same way. The results of ITL were substantiated by its data and the program lasted as long as the principal was at the school.

FIVE

Reflections

ILT had a successful year and as the year came to an end the team met to review the entire experience. In this chapter we will discuss the review. The team was proud because ILT had accomplished its goals and once again the importance of sound, seminal research was validated. ILT can teach many lessons about the successful implementation of any innovation, using research as a roadmap. At that moment the team wanted to recap the details of the journey, creating a blueprint for similar situations.

Because the people who execute the program are in the classroom, teachers should be treated as professionals who might make better decisions than someone farther from the day-to-day operations of the school. Unfortunately, teachers are resigned to classrooms and must follow mandates. Even when they try to produce data, it is ignored and data from standardized tests is used only to pinpoint failing schools and teachers. Instead of receiving support, failing schools are at risk of closures or being reconstituted. ILT chose to focus on the effective use of ongoing formative data in the classroom during instruction.

At the inception of most reform or change programs there is a sense of uncertainty; where should one begin and which direction should the program take? Knowing the research that supports a reform project and being able to ask the right questions are vital. It is important to acknowledge that school reform begins and ends with the goal of student learning and, as such, the questions examined after reading *School as the Home of the Mind* can be the roadmap for any reform project involving teaching and learning.

A comprehensive-needs assessment must be done before attempting any systemic changes. The team did not have the opportunity to do a needs-based assessment but received guidance from the research description of the needs of students who are deemed at-risk. That was a safe starting point. In addition, an assessment must be made of the degree to which the school meets or does not meet the academic, emotional, and social needs of all the students. Specific goals must be generated from the assessment. However, innovation requires the design of specific goals to address existing situations in the environment in which it will function.

These goals must be stated explicitly. ILT had four overarching goals:

1. Student achievement (homework completion, attendance, grades, and attitudes toward school)
2. Post–high school goal setting (work or college)
3. Acceptable social behaviors
4. Parent involvement

The goals also provided the framework by which ILT's success would be assessed.

There is no doubt that any change to the status quo in the school will affect everyone: the district, practitioners, students, parents, and the community. Initially, there is fear, doubt, and a real concern about doing work that was the responsibility of someone who worked for the district, as was the case with ILT. But existing data can be compelling and the validation of decisions through research can crumble the wall of resistance to generate a collaborative, collegial environment, as it was for ILT. Besides, since it is difficult to teach cooperative learning without exhibiting cooperative behavior, the practitioners grew professionally.

In the case of ILT, the team had four weeks before the start of school to develop the program. Their determination overcame all obstacles, doubt, and fear. There was also an element of patience coupled with the time provided to plan. Through time and patience team members had the opportunity to shed their limited thinking and create a vision well beyond the classroom to help all students. That vision included adjustments to the schedule to allow for a common planning time. The principal giving approval to the planning time demonstrated that he had a deep sense of trust with respect to the team members.

The existing collaborative spirit created an environment of sharing that was nonexistent in the traditional school culture. When the best possible lesson was designed, that lesson was placed in a file, accessible to everyone. Every lesson was planned in such a way that it gave students a compelling reason to examine the content. It was related to life or a career and definitely tied to previous learning. Lessons were designed to improve test taking, critical thinking, problem-solving skills, study skills, note taking, time management, and writing skills.

As much as lesson plans can capture the interactions in the classes, the methods of instruction should be germane to the program holistically. It is very important to note that the lesson plans should be thoughtful and cohesive, not isolated and fragmented. All students read the same material but an intentional connection was made to the students' ambitions. For example, in language arts, the story *Twelve Angry Men* gave aspiring correctional officers the opportunity to craft a police report on a crime scene and future journalists were given the opportunity to describe the crime scene (based on what the jurors said). All others wrote a persuasive essay to convince the last juror to vote along with the others.

Collaborative lesson planning promoted a writing assignment with two grades. For example, an essay on the Civil War would earn one grade in social studies (content specific) and another grade in language arts, assessed for incorporating writing mechanics that required improvement, as cited in the writing assessment report.

Whatever change is decided on, it must pervade all aspects of the program. Words such as collaboration and learning organization were quite prevalent in ILT. Therefore, change in ILT resided in more than just lesson design and instruction. Collaboration was exemplified in ILT through regular classroom observations by peers for the purpose of constructive feedback and improvement. Respect for the expertise of other colleagues was vital, which became evident in the frank discussions about the appropriateness of the strategy. An increasing sense of self-efficacy pervaded the lesson planning sessions in ILT.

Individual classrooms became laboratories and, as true risk-takers, educators practiced and reflected on the learning environment in the classroom. This result was no surprise, as research affirms that teachers who develop a sense of efficacy based on sound practice and knowledge actually improve their professional skills.

Change also affects roles and responsibilities. Committed educators ran professional development meetings, met with parents regularly, and engaged in casual conversations that moved from griping to discussing student's needs and the role of pedagogy in teaching. But it is impossible to teach a concept without learning it. Educators, novice or expert, would now have to learn to infuse critical thinking, problem-solving skills, and life and social skills into the curriculum.

The principal's role changed from administrator to enabler of a reform program, and one of true instructional leadership. The principal enabled the team to demonstrate leadership in charting the course of the program. A monthly report and requests for assistance for the things they could not control were the only requests from the principal. Both the union and the principal exhibited a collaborative approach to the processes that ILT requested. No program will survive without strong support from the decision makers.

The principal in this case was supportive of the team and out of necessity took a take-charge approach because there was no time for the district to identify the students and then propose a plan. The academic school year would have been in session by then and corrective actions, which are best implemented at the beginning of the year, would have seemed ill-placed.

Having the principal's support for these beliefs is desirable for any endeavor. The principal took bold steps to get approval for resources, such as reduced workloads, a block of rooms, and a work space. Such actions created a group of individuals committed to student welfare and success. There was an understanding that the students' success was also that of the team members in the program.

Having the support of the principal and the union made it easy to change policy to support ILT. The nature of ILT called for a change in the evaluation process. A letter justifying the ratings was added to the process. Mandated daily homework assignments were relaxed in order to be aligned with the recommendations of the research. Working on the premise that homework is not "left over" but used to "practice," be "interactive," or connect school and the world, the homework policy was adjusted.

When student learning is the focus, anything is possible; people can go through personal change as well. Some ingrained habits can stymie the program. Contractually, teachers had five personal days and ten sick days. Personal days were lost if not taken during the school year. Many teachers stood to lose personal days and, by the end of the year, would seek to recoup those days. Such actions at year end could adversely affect student performance on the final exams. That year, ILT members lost personal days and dedicated those days to review for finals with their students.

In addition, providing incentives for the students was important. In ILT there was an extra credit system (see appendix K) that required instructors to be present and developed into a friendly competition among classes. Students were determined that their class would have the highest number of students with perfect attendance. Their excitement transcended to the class-level and soon the students were collaboratively working to make their class victorious. There was a sense of motivation and personal responsibility to be in class every day.

The discussion on motivation in the research considers extrinsic motivation, and these inexpensive gestures—even simply recognizing the students, their parents, and the teachers in the ILT Newsletter—generated lots of motivation to fulfill the new policies and procedures. Perfect attendance allowed for only one absence for the month, and there had to be a good reason provided for that absence. The friendly competition that evolved was another social skill that was not an initial goal of ILT, but was beneficial to the students.

Setting goals also motivates individuals. For ILT students, looking forward to a job after having earned good grades had to be a motivator, as could being exposed to the college fairs and career assemblies and then having a conversation with a parent and the guidance counselor about post–high school goals. The plan was laid out and the students merely needed to embrace the opportunities to be successful. Parents were appreciative of this service and were happy they were treated as partners, and not simply for as fund-raisers.

A successful reform program must include life skills. Most students developed a sense of competence when they learned or honed their life skills. Those who worked learned how to balance a checkbook and manage money. They felt a sense of accomplishment. The Small Business Association did presentations for those who wanted to own a business and would have to apply for a small business loan. In addition, all students were exposed to the process of filing taxes. ILT students were being prepared for life—the ultimate goal of education.

At-risk students cannot succeed alone and are usually too timid to ask for assistance. Support systems must be included, even if is just the teacher in the classroom. ILT had a team of teachers. Therefore, in ILT, the asking was done by someone else, not the student. The Peer Leaders and members of the National Honor Society, who needed credit points for community service requirements, offered tutoring and baby-sitting services. Most ILT students availed themselves of the services. There is no doubt that these services supported student success but the school does not always have these resources. Therefore, the social services of eye specialists, psychologists, and the Youth Multi-Service Centers were also made available for ILT students.

Effective change must be cost-effective. Usually, when an educator is absent, a substitute teacher is hired. The collaborative relationships in ILT and the structure of the program had the added bonus of doing away with the need for substitutes. Classes could be combined or supervised by other team members if a teacher were absent. This was a cost-saving benefit and, more importantly, a benefit that prevented an interruption in instruction because the team member could re-teach and enforce rather than supervise seatwork.

Schools are used to having department chairs and team leaders who serve as the conduits for the principal or a supervisor in the district office. The role of the facilitator was relatively new at that time, but today, with the dawn of teacher-leaders, training and support will be more forthcoming. This facilitator, unlike a department chair, helped develop the program, conducted professional development activities, acted as a liaison to the outside community, submitted monthly reports to the principal, and had to be versed in some aspects of the research. Presently, the ETS has spearheaded the development of Teacher Leader Standards.

ILT was as much about student achievement as it was about professional growth. It was about changing cultures: moving from an individualistic culture, like that exhibited in traditional schools, to one of collegiality and collaboration. Note that in a traditional culture, having friends at school does not take away the environment of competition that exists. ILT resided in a traditional culture. Belief systems of traditional schools usually exhibit no tolerance for methodical trial and error as a means to success. An approach to change often fails to acknowledge that practitioners need time to practice new skills before expecting substantial shifts in habits and routines.

There is a difference between traditional groups and professional groups. A major characteristic of traditional group culture is competition, clouded by concerns for individual rewards and existing for a short duration. In contrast, professional groups are ongoing, exhibiting a culture of collaboration and interdependence with a sense of individual accountability where everyone is a learner.

That culture translated into the ways ILT teachers interacted with parents. Parents too became learners and partners in their children's education. Because successful reform cannot occur without parental support, in collaboration with the guidance department and community psychologists, ILT offered mediation services between the parent and child. Several relationships were mended through this process.

Suspicion and mistrust were replaced by a caring family atmosphere. Initially, students disliked the close monitoring of attendance and frequent communication with parents (see appendix L). But despite a sense of disequilibrium in a new environment, gradually there was a growing sense of self-efficacy and a sense of confidence in the majority of students, including the sixteen students who moved to the eleventh grade. The lesson here was that academic improvement is a viable goal but will not be actualized without social and emotional supports.

Addressing the nonacademic needs of the students offered a nurturing, caring environment. Offering student services, such as eye exams, summer job placements, counseling with psychologists, and introducing students to the breakfast program, addressed needs that, once taken care of, would support their learning. Consideration of cultural differences cemented the bond between ILT and the parents.

One example of the success the ILT program fostered was seen in the case of several Hispanic parents who had difficulty understanding the teachers. To help them, the bilingual department sent a representative to the meetings. In addition, that department assisted these students with assignments and provided clarification on the employment process for eligible Hispanic students who qualified for the job program. Combined, approximately 250 students, including Hispanics, went through the job program.

The local education policy, as well as existing research by Brandt (1998), recommends that change agents need to know their social and political environment. There were instances in which knowledge of the social and political setting proved extremely valuable.

For example, when parents did not show up for meetings or to pick up report cards, one conclusion might be that they do not care. However, this was simply a case of finances, because most parents would lose pay for any time taken away from their job. A senator and a lawyer from the legislature confirmed that employers were required to give employees time to go to their child's school, without loss of pay. All that was required was a form of documentation that the parent had visited the school. This information was included in the newsletter so parents would be aware of it.

Upon arrival at the school, every parent signed in and out at the registrar's office. The slip indicated arrival and departure times and carried the school's seal. Once back on the job, parents could submit this document to their employer. Within two months, most of the parents came to the meetings and established relationships with the team.

In addition, ILT made certain activities easy for parents that in the traditional culture would require parents to make appointments with every teacher individually. During report card distribution, for example, all team members were brought to the same location, along with the guidance counselors and an individual from the bilingual department (if interpretive services were needed) so parents could have easy access to all the adults who supported their child. Eventually the host school brought all teachers to the gym; that way parents did not have to walk the entire campus to visit all their children's teachers.

When individuals sense that someone cares, they are more willing to support others' endeavors. With a small business grant, the PTA ran Saturday Academies in the core subject areas to help parents become proficient enough to better assist their child. ILT students could attend with their parents. Most parents attended, since baby-sitting services were offered by the National Honor Society. Giving guidance on homework, coupled with the Saturday Academies, raised the level of homework completion to nearly 80 percent by the end of the school year. This validated the research that found that when families are involved, students achieve.

Communication is the key if a program is to be successful. Communicating frequently with the parents and soliciting their assistance in the decision-making process of ILT as well as in their child's future solidified the partnership. Making the rules and expectations explicitly known at the beginning of the year, followed by phone calls, weekly progress reports, and recognition in the monthly newsletters for more than just academics, gave a more holistic view of student progress than the traditional methods parents were used to. ILT parents did not come to the school to disrespect adults on the campus but to assist, provide support, and offer suggestions.

Without a sense of commitment, reform programs will remain compelling only on paper. The teachers in ILT were not offered tangible or monetary incentives. The team's experience was testimony to the validity of research that states that just as important as incentive is giving members the opportunity to share and to experience professional learning opportunities that help them perform their jobs better (Brandt, 1998).

Significant improvements in students begin with the retooling of teachers through a knowledge and understanding of the research, a shared vision, and an agreed-upon pedagogical approach. Trust and personal sacrifices are as important as research and pedagogy. Emphasis on the social and emotional context for everyone was integral to the type of relationships that were formed. Challenges moved the process, and no matter what successes were experienced, continual assessments and adjustments were made.

Retooling educators is paramount to building their self-efficacy in teaching. In a brief survey at the end of the second semester, the team was asked to rate personal comfort levels on a scale of one to five, with five being the highest. The ratings were matched to the achievement levels of the students in the classes. There was a strong alignment. It was quite noticeable that high levels of comfort yielded more As and Bs. Lower levels had Bs, Cs, and a few Fs. This analysis was used as a self-reflection tool; these teachers now understood the effect of their level of confidence on student learning.

One's belief system and comfort level with any process affects student outcome. The way the team felt about ILT can be summed up by the following responses given by team members at the end of the year:

> ILT made me understand how essential peer collaboration is for meaningful lesson planning and professional development. It demonstrated that lessons could be interdisciplinary without losing the essence of the content. It also taught me the importance of administrative support for any innovation. (C. M., educator in ILT, interviewed June 1991)

> Adding the dimension of extended activities to our lesson plans, where the content had to be applied to a real world situation, gave relevance to my teaching. (S. S., educator in ILT, interviewed June 1991)

Schools exist to educate the next generation of citizens and the success of innovations that support student achievement requires complementary systemic changes in the education system. Current structures can stymie the success of innovations just as certain policies and guidelines can limit teachers' use of data to make instructional adjustments and design ongoing formative assessments. For example, due to privacy laws, student records are not easily accessible, even though this information could make programs more effective. Sometimes it takes an unpleasant incident for the information to be released.

Successful endeavors such as ILT are always at risk of being influenced by unpleasant variables that can negatively affect any program. No matter how noble the cause, change agents cannot escape professional jealousy. All the aspects of school life addressed through ILT did not earn the group praises from other school staff personnel. The fact that school violence in the tenth grade was down considerably went unrecognized. No student from ILT was involved in an altercation during their years at the school. Fifteen of the sixteen students graduated without repeating a class. One student left before the end of the year for Job Corps.

Those in the business of change must accept failure as a signal for corrective action. There should be no standard, curriculum, test, or strategy that is so fixed that when it does not produce results, the user is blamed and opportunities for change are dismissed. Change, when made in the best interest of those it serves, has produced notable outcomes.

Despite setbacks, persistence breeds success. In the end, the questions that provided the foundation for ILT can now be favorably answered. The team was clear on the purpose and use of research. The changes needed in curriculum and instruction were unambiguous and the changes to be made by the school had been identified. ILT began with a small issue that had a big impact. It could have been easy to schedule the students with the four teachers and do nothing else, but factors such as poor nutrition, low motivation, high absenteeism, and the noncompletion of homework would have undermined any goals set for the students.

Since ILT, many elements have been introduced in the education process. Technology has provided a means to educate a vast number of students when there is a shortage of teachers. Technology has its place in the information age but there is a need for caution. If the goal is to develop a collaborative community of learners, technology yields a different type of dynamic. Having to type responses may limit the scope of the discussion compared to that of a face to face. It will be interesting to see employees in the workplace whose main form of interaction is the computer or other technical devices.

In education, a results-oriented approach coupled with an objective way of measuring progress has led to a focus on testing. For high school it was the SATs and meeting a benchmark called Average Yearly Progress (AYP). When passing rates began to drop nationally, a focus was placed on teachers' end-of-year evaluations, which would now be based on how many of the students passed the class. Failure to meet standards over five years exposed schools to a progress continuum that started with a warning and could end up with the possibility of the school being closed.

High failure rates have not gone unnoticed and neither has the fact that the needs of students are not being met. The program *Understanding by Design* (Wiggins and McTighe, 2005) sought to address the idea of *teacher as designer* as it pertained to lesson designs. These lessons should be aligned to curriculum and standards but more importantly they should consider the social and emotional aspects of the child as well as their rate of learning. Differentiation would be the method of assigning tasks.

Other research designs gave teachers a method of determining the "big ideas" of the curriculum to ensure a coherent teaching process of the concepts. This means that the textbook may not be taught in the sequence of the chapters nor the established curriculum. The best part of the lesson design processes was to ensure that students are aware of the curriculum map. The curriculum map outlines the main concepts students will learn and all the concepts that fit into the groups. Students have a coherent view of the curriculum and are aware of the connections.

Schools are really trying to address student failure but most programs introduced to address failure usually address one thing. Supporting factors are not considered. For example, several schools trying to move away from the status quo have introduced block scheduling as a way to handle the swelling curriculum. If nothing else was changed to receive this innovation, the success of the program might be limited.

Others introduced interdisciplinary teams as prescribed by the research. The only caution is that some themes were "forced" and some themes were year-round. Attempts to make learning relevant to the student's world saw the implementation of project-based and service learning and attempts at a family-type setting saw the creation of advisory periods or, on a more elaborate scale, "houses." There is no doubt that the quest for improving education has been an ongoing challenge. Every step of the way, there has been an attempt to improve education, but each time the innovation was seen as the "magic bullet."

Most recently (2011), the Common Core State Standards have been worked on. But the standards, no matter how well written, will not increase student learning just because they exist. These standards will have to be written in a way both students and teachers can understand and lots of professional development will be needed to support teachers and this environment that may require new instructional methods. Again the success of any innovation is dependent on the preparedness of the environment to receive it. What will need to change for the Common Core State Standards to be successful?

One observation of educational innovations was that each program or process was introduced without much change to the environment in which the innovation was going to function. As a result, many innovations showed some progress but would have achieved much more if the setting and other elements of the environment had responded to the change.

SUMMARY

Reform should not be just about grades. Students may achieve, but more important, changes in the environment should support that success; for example, a caring environment where all stakeholders play a part in nurturing the individual. Effective reform should support career choices and groom students to be productive citizens. The end result then should not be just about grades but about the fulfillment of aspirations and dreams. Reform that focuses just on grades misses the mark.

Several theories have been introduced into education since this experience, yet the search continues to find ways to assist students. One thing is certain, there is no magic bullet. Changing only one aspect of any environment seldom yields the success intended. Innovations in education must always consider the educational climate and the "whole child."

SIX

Words of Wisdom

Change begins with an urgent need. The impetus for change that led to the development and implementation of ILT was school safety. But addressing that one issue resulted in the identification of additional factors that needed to be addressed. Change agents should be cognizant of the fact that addressing one factor in education may require additional adjustments elsewhere.

Successful changes in education have a research base that drives decisions on those changes, and that was the case with ILT. Although the principal suggested placing all the at-risk students in one class, the team was able to point to research that strongly advocates just the opposite. Had the principal placed all the students in one class, the students would continue to exhibit behaviors that are detrimental to academic performance and in some instances escalate those negative behaviors. It is extremely important that any educator who assumes a leadership role that requires curriculum and/or systemic organization changes have a solid foundation in educational research.

The caution here with regard to research is that existing research that is tried and true should not be dismissed for more recent research without first establishing the seminal nature of the new research. In short, "new" should not be the operating factor.

Changing mindsets can be a real challenge—especially in the case of teachers who may not see any need to change or learn something new. However, a facilitator who creates a comfortable atmosphere as a group embarks on a quest of unfamiliar roles is an asset to any change process. This sense of comfort and support is critical to the experiences individuals will have and ultimately the types of outcomes the program will have.

Educators in ILT went outside the delineated scope of their work and considered nutrition and other nonacademic issues as part of the education process. Having accomplished the goals set for ILT, the educators never looked at another student as a failure, and as a result, the approach to teaching and learning changed. The stark reality is that one cannot implement a breakfast program, change nothing else, and expect a rapid turnaround on student success.

One of the keys to a successful change process is being able to convince others that together they can develop a viable solution. Equally important—and challenging—is the ability to motivate one's colleagues to try something new that is not on anyone's radar. ILT was a success. It met its goals of increasing student learning, reducing absenteeism, teaching social skills, and facilitating critical thinking with varying rates of success. But it would not have been so successful without principal support, cooperation, and a changed school culture within the program.

Success requires a visionary principal. The principal must be able to detail a morally compelling vision of student learning, teaching, leadership, and professional development that motivates a team to engage in the change process. Under such leadership, teams can have the time, support, and patience to try nontraditional methods, be at ease with risk-taking, and still be held accountable.

Such vision must identify policies, resources, and changes necessary to support reform. It must encompass many entities in education and address areas such as district accountability, school schedules, calendars, and, at times, collective-bargaining agreements. The fact that educational change does not always begin at the district level, and that one can't always wait for all facets to be in place to begin, is central to the change process.

Everyone on the team must understand the goal so the appropriate research can be identified. There are times when the goal is not clear. For example, ILT began with a focus on school safety and went on to include academic and social well-being—a much broader picture. Getting to the big picture is important since there are secondary factors that can affect the success of the change process.

Leaders should be able to not only articulate the goals of the reform program but have a sense of the type of individuals needed to make it a success. In this case, a selection process was of lesser importance to the desired attributes of the individuals who would be part of the process. Based on the attributes, the department chairs identified the members of ILT. The selected teachers were a good choice and proved that the status of veteran or novice did not matter; what mattered was one's ability to effect change. These veterans had demonstrated effectiveness in teaching, exhibited empathy for students, and were not shy about going the extra mile to help students succeed.

Applying new concepts in an old framework can be disastrous. Better to implement the new approach on its own merit than try to integrate old and new, especially when it appears forced. Well-planned processes in a supportive environment can prevail in an "inadequate" system and effect some change. However, a hostile environment will negatively impact any innovation.

ILT created its own system within a system. Perhaps that is why it was able to survive, even though the parent or host system continued to operate under the old rules. This was an instance of small changes applied at the points that would realize the greatest leverage, producing noticeable results. Research should drive actions in education, but change agents and reformers need to be cognizant of the fact that the research isn't always available in one study. Sometimes an eclectic approach to identifying relevant studies is necessary.

Evaluation at the end of initial implementation supports continuation or termination of a program. In addition, continuous assessment and appropriate adaptations based on findings are recommended. Along with these assessments come trust and the acceptance that mistakes will be made and all that is needed is corrective action.

Continuous assessment will permit ongoing adjustments to any program. However, practices that have proven to work in the past should not be dismissed for something new without a convincing reason. Success at best can be incremental: significant enough but very slow. Either way, change agents, the district, or those in charge need to exercise patience with any new process. Research shows that it takes a business venture five years to post significant results. In education, sadly, the trend is to dismiss after the first year.

Education will thrive if those closest to the students are allowed to create visions of success for them. School personnel are not in a position to conduct the level of scientific research that the research world demands. However, if this process had not occurred, then 483 lives, and certainly those of the 16 students, would not have been touched in such a manner.

When this educational process (ILT) was implemented, terms such as *curriculum mapping, backwards mapping, teacher leader, mentors, coaches, formative assessment, accountability, standards,* and *job-embedded professional development* did not dominate the lingo of the educational world as it does now. Years ago, it was *team teaching, block scheduling, master educator, evaluation, accountability,* and the creation of *houses.* These are different names but some have similar meanings. For example, *master teacher* performs duties similar to that of a *mentor* while *team teaching* has similar attributes of interdisciplinary teaching.

Truancy, low academic performance, unaligned curricula, and low achievement levels still plague education. Encouraging is the reality that there is much more research today to support the innovation designed by these four teachers and the facilitator.

Another key to success is the understanding that professional development is not an event; it is a process and it is most rewarding when tied explicitly to student learning. Being exposed to a concept in a workshop setting only one time does not guarantee the information will be used. However, if at the job setting the concept is either discussed in teams or tried in the classrooms with an examination of results, there is a strong possibility that the learning will improve one's proficiency with the concept and spark interest in other related concepts. Learning should be a lifelong endeavor and teachers should be provided with ongoing opportunities to serve as models to students.

When a program is successful, educators must identify resources to sustain it. Such continuity effects change in school culture and deepens the practitioners' intrapersonal reflection process and group collaboration skills, which have profound effects on instruction, student learning, and individual professional development growth plans.

At all stages of the change process, the voices of the stakeholders are important. Any medium that helps students and individuals express themselves in a way that produces constructive feedback is essential. A survey (see appendix L) of the students to get feedback on ILT revealed that at another school, a program called Focus 27 for truant and belligerent students existed, but had led to labeling and teasing. The team concluded that the downfall of Focus 27 was that it grouped all the failing students into one program and "watered down" the curriculum—the very thing the team dissuaded the principal from doing. A list of the students' top responses can be found in appendix L.

All programs require funding. Acquiring funding from multiple sources helps strengthen and sustain the program. Even when the program does not have the amount of money a project of this magnitude requires, in-kind resources can provide much-needed supplemental resources.

When embarking on an innovation in education reform such as ILT, one should ask several questions:

- What do you know about the students for whom the program is being developed?
- How should the curriculum be structured?
- How will instruction be delivered?
- What schools and classrooms need to be included in the education reform?
- How will the impact of the program be evaluated?

It is important to ask the right questions. The examination of the research was not to simply validate the behavior of the at-risk child, but to investigate what the research identified as the needs of the at-risk child. The overriding question considered by the team was: "What is lacking in the lives of at-risk students that contributes to their conduct and poor academic performance?" The response to that question provided the vision and the process of ILT.

Another key point is that team effort guarantees that the work will get done. In addition, having a facilitator on the team ensures the administrative tasks will get done. If not, the other team members will view such activities as an add-on to already burdened workloads. Also, to ensure that tasks are done well, the allotted planning time should be made sufficient to accomplish instructional planning, parent meetings, professional development, and the completion of administrative tasks.

The professional development experiences must be well-planned. Even if the session is a one-time workshop, the content should be relevant and participants should be able to implement the information the next day in the classroom. Content for the sessions should never be guided by the latest, most popularly advertised research. Successful sessions must be job-embedded, ongoing, and provide room for reflection.

Parent involvement must be defined as more than a numbers game. Picking up a report card demonstrates fulfillment of parental responsibilities, but being involved calls for time, planning, and a display of genuine interest that goes beyond what is expected. For example, assisting with post–high school plans is more than identifying funds and speaking with the guidance department. Such planning requires interacting with the children and knowing what their goals are so that appropriate recommendations will be forthcoming.

Successful programs should help build parent efficacy. Engaging parents in the Saturday Academies program that builds their own self-efficacy and in planning for their child's college process made parents aware of what ILT was attempting to achieve. The impression made on parents was so strong that when forces moved to eliminate the program, it was the parents who stood up for ILT.

Change may involve the need for additional services. Whatever services are required, the change agents must be able to locate and direct those in need of these services to the right place. Many nonacademic services have a profound effect on student learning. Yet, very rarely are those services placed in the equation when teachers are assessed based on their students' performances.

To raise the bar without putting supports in place for additional services will simply frustrate teachers and inhibit progress. ILT was a true school-within-a-school effort. It was important to collaborate with almost every group in the school: guidance, bilingual, school monitors, the school nurse, and even the cafeteria workers. In the community, there was collaboration with groups like the Vision Center, which assessed the students' need for glasses and the business community that provided the summer jobs.

Other supports for ILT included schedule and work load adjustments and the motivational opportunities made available to the students. Support must be given to both students and educators or attempts to make changes will not be taken seriously and therefore nothing will improve.

At least the support given to both teachers and students to create a sense of family, accomplished by the annexed classes, was a good start.

Change does not come easily. Even when the education policy of the district suggests that the system should be aware of its social setting and adjust as those settings change, any steps taken to actualize this policy is met with resistance. No matter how well-intentioned, even when there is proof that student learning and disposition have improved, the actions of change agents will be deemed as self-serving. Resistance plays a pivotal role in the change process as ingrained mental models confront new roles.

In this new era, the recommendations of the SCANS Report about having a workforce that can problem solve and work together, are essential. No one should work in isolation. Learning communities create shared responsibility in looking at student work, refining instruction, and assessment. Schools with professional communities set high standards for students and use authentic pedagogy to improve instruction.

Change agents should take time to plan but acknowledge that there will be occasions when there is insufficient time to do so. Weigh the consequences of inaction and if it is costly, seize the moment. Be mindful that even when grade summary reports indicate success, the cynicism of others will not subside. Whenever opportunity arises to make a difference in student learning and school culture, don't hesitate—start wherever possible.

At times, it is the decision of a new superintendent or principal to dismiss existing programs and infuse something new. As a result, it becomes difficult to take research-based programs seriously because "this too shall pass." The team's experience suggests that it is imperative that any new processes introduced in schools that can aid students' needs to be viewed as a process to be sustained and improved over time with the support of the district regardless of who is in charge. Notably, the most successful reform is both school- and district-wide.

There is much more research today to support work for at-risk students. It is a fact that both students and teachers will undergo a sense of discomfort as they go through change; in the educational world it is called *cognitive dissonance*. To help address this dissonance, change agents must have the resources, such as professional development, to support the change process.

Ann Lieberman and Lynne Miller (1999) endorse the findings of decades of research; successful reform requires certain conditions. One condition attends to the needs of both students and teachers. For teachers, both personal and professional needs should be addressed. Another condition is the availability of resources including professional development and other support structures. Schools engaged in the process of reform need to create an environment for learning for students as well as teachers.

Bruce Joyce and Beverly Showers (1995), after an in-depth review of research and best practices in staff development, stress the fact that a characteristic common to successful schools is that they have targeted and specific student-learning goals. The procedures used to develop and support those goals are backed by sound research findings. One procedure these schools use is the conducting of formative and summative assessments to measure student learning outcomes.

These studies indicate that there was a substantial amount of professional development with the understanding that the goal-based initiatives required teacher and student learning of new procedures. In addition, in those schools, data was regularly collected and disseminated in a timely manner so that staff could use the findings to inform their instruction.

Bruce and Showers (1995) outlined the need for regular assessment, data collection and dissemination, and clearly marked learning goals and professional development.

But they also stressed the need for companionship, today referred to as *teams* or *professional learning communities (PLCs)*. Simply put, the researchers emphasize the power of collaboration by suggesting that the relationships developed through teams or professional learning communities could influence people to change behaviors they would not otherwise, were it not for these relationships.

Important to PLC success is ownership of the process and functions. Very often, teachers are not involved in decisions made about education. However, almost all these decisions require teachers to make changes or adjustments to their lesson plans and instruction. As a result, there may be less *buy-in* to the changes, and even less understanding of what is being required and which complexities of the task need to be addressed.

James Stigler and James Hiebert (1999) support the view that educators need to be involved in the decision-making and fulfill the decisions as a team. The researchers maintain that successful reform efforts employ a collaborative approach. The benefit of the collaborative efforts of *teams* or, more recently, *professional learning communities* is well documented in the research literature.

Certainly, group work teaches many social skills, regardless of who is involved, but the learning that results is phenomenal, and research affirms that collaborative behaviors on the part of teachers is emulated by the students who observe their modeling (Johnson and Johnson, 1998; Smith and Scott, 1990). If school reform can entail groups freed from restrictions and working towards a goal and not just individuals complying with a mandate, then the positive results will be greater.

Kenneth W. Eastwood and Karen Seashore Louis (1992) avow that a collaborative environment has been found to be the single most important factor for successful school reform (pp. 213–15). Melanie Morrison and D'Ette (2000) confirm that increased student learning was inextricably tied to teacher learning and collaboration.

There is no question that school culture has always been resistant to change. The research strongly affirms that a facet of effective school change is that of cooperation coupled with an environment where both teachers and students are learners. One of the areas in which schools will have to do much more is to move with the times, heeding the findings of research. Presently, a lot of attention has been given to the brain. Application of the research findings to classroom and school practice is still very controversial, yet everyone agrees on the role of the brain in learning.

However, through the work of David H. Rose, cofounder and chief education officer at CAST and a doctoral student at Harvard, the Universal Design for Learning (UDL) has developed guidelines the goal of which is to help teachers master the process of learning. To reach this goal, UDL provides teachers with a framework for understanding how to reshape curriculum to meet the needs of all learners.

In teaching UDL, teachers understand how the brain works and focus on the "what" of learning. This focuses on our ability to identify or gather information. They also focus on the "how" of learning. That means the teacher has to consider that everyone learns differently and therefore allow students to demonstrate mastery in different ways. In addition, the framework examines the "why" of learning which concentrates on the educator's ability to motivate students and sustain their love for learning.

The problems and hindrances are still evident everywhere and many conversations about solutions are still fragmented and sometimes cyclical. One lesson learned from ILT is that for any reform to be highly effective it must be as comprehensive as it can be. Otherwise, change agents will tinker with systems in a piecemeal fashion and the domino effect down the road will have negative repercussions.

SUMMARY

The program described in this book occurred in the 1991–1992 school year and continued for several years after. Presently, the program is not being used since most of the individuals who were engaged in the program have left the school, including the principal. However, the support given by the principal, the district, and the local union was phenomenal.

The concept of *dated research* should provide pause to educators. Most research provides room for further research; sometimes a meta-analysis of existing research creates new insight or a new program. The goal should be an awareness of what exists and before applying research to the task, the goal should be to determine whether the research *old* and *new* has passed the litmus test: "Has it been tried?" and "Is it true?" The habit of promoting a research study as the magic bullet is misleading. All students cannot be taught in the same way and before interventions are implemented, knowledge about those students is critical to the design of the intervention.

Many schools have gone beyond academics to help students achieve. Various research concepts have been applied to help students achieve. For example, depending on your age the following, with similar attributes and some differences, become important: *teams, team teaching, site-based management, school improvement teams,* and now *professional learning communities.* Similarly, there is *looping, houses,* and *academies* all with the same goal in mind: linking the social aspects of learning and academics. Several have been effective but in most cases the additional supports were nonexistent.

The toughest thing to accept, for many, is that the local union had a mission not only to improve the conditions in which their members work but, more importantly, help them do their jobs better through professional development. In fact, many unionized organizations provide professional development for their members. The simple message to be shared from the ILT experience is that when the well-being of students is at risk, the call is to action and the development of reform that supports student learning and the attainment of their dreams.

SEVEN

From Then to Now

This book could not conclude without reference to research. In the education world, there is a push for new research—and rightly so. Often, that push results in basic research being expanded and given a new name or packaged in a more appealing way. By exposing those in education to as much research as possible, we promote deeper and broader knowledge of research concepts.

One needs only to enter "Bloom's taxonomy" in a search engine to be amazed at the various versions and interpretations of the same concept. Today, everyone seems to approach Bloom's taxonomy as levels of "thinking" when in fact he designed the taxonomy as levels of tasks (not types of questions) to assess the growth of the students with special needs with whom he was working. Educators have been misled about Bloom's taxonomy.

Several current works have tried to move from the hierarchical model of thinking with questionable success. These models do not indicate that when crafting a response to a question, all facets of the taxonomy are utilized. For example, one cannot evaluate without knowledge, comprehension, analysis, and synthesis coupled with the appropriate critical thinking skills. As a matter of fact, the cognitive scientists make it clear that knowledge and comprehension are a given when it comes to thinking and responding to questions. Simply put, students are unable to respond to questions on content they have not learned.

Depending on one's age, the terms professional learning communities, site-based management teams, and school improvement teams may be more or less familiar. Despite the differing titles, these groups function in similar ways in schools with a few differences. The goal for each one is to identify areas needing improvement in the school and develop a course of action to address these areas.

ILT considered the research with regard to discipline. Some of the older research supported pullout programs; the newer research did not, strongly opposing the sequestering of the students. Rather than addressing the behavior, the ILT program addressed the underlying deterrents to the students' success. Simply following a discipline-based program did not seem to meet all the needs of most of the students. It seemed that the relationship of trust had to be established before students adhered to a rigid discipline plan or routine.

Many researchers have discussed motivating students by making the curriculum relevant. Studies point to programs such as integrated learning, Project Zero, project-based learning, and content-area fairs as ways to do this. Today we have the Common Core State Standards collaboratively assembling what students should know and be able to do at all grade levels. These standards are much needed and perhaps well outlined, but again, when it comes to the students in the classroom, the best designed lesson plans will not be able to overcome the nonacademic influences that negatively affect student learning.

One theme in this book is collaboration. That term existed in education research starting in the 1970s, yet there are only pockets of collaboration in schools. Very often, when an innovation is introduced, only those assigned to the project are involved. In ILT the collaboration went beyond the teachers in the program. Every staff member who was able to enhance the students' experience was included—the monitors, the Guidance Department, the cafeteria workers, and the nurse—making ILT a holistic program and not one that focused simply on behavior and academics.

It is important to note that many schools have implemented innovations to assist student learning with very little funding. This book seeks to answer the question, "Can a school explore changes that require little funding but if done correctly can have a big impact on the 'whole child?'" On August 30, 2011, a blog post by Ken Kay on *Edutopia* identified four "Cs" that schools should implement in order to achieve twentieth-century schools. These are:

- Critical Thinking
- Communication
- Collaboration
- Creativity

These skills are no different from some of the ones mentioned in SCANS and incorporated in ILT. Hopefully schools will take on the challenge of using content to teach skills rather than teaching content to pass tests.

Research on leadership examined several management styles. In the past, the role of the employee was to follow directions. As time progressed, businesses were asking for employees who could work with others and problem-solve. The latter best described the ILT process. Educators were treated as professionals being given the freedom to solve problems at the school level. More importantly the problems dealt with content, instruction, and student learning.

The role of the principal or leaders cannot be overstated. Volumes of research have focused on the role of leadership as it relates to business or reforming schools. Excellent leaders embrace change and sometimes are the change agents. When innovations do not yield expected results, an attribute of a good leader is to engage in a discussion to examine what went wrong and where improvements could be made, not to administer punishment. Recent research on leadership calls for managers to be involved but not micromanage.

USING LESSONS LEARNED

Teachers can use the research, resources, and experiences shared in this book to implement change in their schools. First, identify the problem to be addressed. Examine causes of the problem—this may help you identify other support structures that will prove helpful. Instead of focusing on the problem, try to get to know the students through a survey, a quiz, an anticipation set, or simple conversation. Whether the school purchases a prepackaged program or develops its own, that program must complement and support the mission and vision of the school, but, more importantly, it must meet the needs of the students.

Then consider how best to implement the program. What are the limitations of the host school that may inhibit the program's success? What factors are sufficient—or required—to guarantee the success of the program? Considering all the responses to these questions, identify what must change in the institution to support the program.

Regardless of how well developed a program is, consultation and professional development are still vital. It is important that the professional development be ongoing and aligned to the needs of those working on the program and those being served by the program.

Another aspect of the program that cannot be ignored is assessment or evaluation. Before launching the program, those involved at the school should determine how the effectiveness of the program will be assessed. The team should be mindful that no students other than those in the program are exposed to its concepts and skills. If the program is implemented schoolwide, the appropriate data for the previous year(s) should be available for comparison. If possible, an outside evaluator may lend credence to the results.

Coordinating all components of new programs requires leadership skills that allow the voices of others to be heard in a way that sends a message that all opinions are valued. Above all, the team should be visionary, continually assessing the program and determining what may need to be adjusted along the way. *Teacher Leader Standards* (2011), published by ETS, is a helpful guide on teacher leadership. This document outlines the types of skills teacher leaders should possess.

Every education innovation is shaped by existing or established research, but research must be ongoing, digging deeper, considering new angles and aspects. By considering research past and present, we have better insight into education reform.

Appendix A

Group Expectations Letter to Parents

October 1, 1991

To the Parents of _____,

It is indeed a pleasure to have your child in our team. Although the school year has already begun, we have altered our plans to develop a learning experience that we believe would better suit your child and make this year an exciting one.

We would like to open the doors of communication with you as we attempt to positively nurture your child. Therefore, this letter seeks to address two concerns:

1. Attendance: Attendance is pivotal to successful completion of high school. Every week we will furnish you with a weekly attendance and grade report.
2. Class Rules: see appendix B

If you have any questions, please contact us at the school, 294/782-9000 or use this mailbox for correspondence:

Educators
St. Cedar High School
Riverdale #2
Stormhill, Bonanza, UG 1111

We look forward to a fruitful year.

Sincerely,
    The Tenth Grade Team

Mr. Jerome Coles	Math
Ms. Anna Labin	Language Arts
Ms. Carla Morales	Social Studies
Mr. Santos Rodriguez	Science

Appendix B

Class Rules

CLASS REQUIREMENTS

Bring to class daily:

- Notebook
- Covered textbooks
- Loose leaves of blank ruled paper
- Black, blue, or red pen and a pencil
- Regular-size folder
- Homework

CLASS RULES

- Attend classes regularly and punctually.
- Five unexcused absences for the quarter will be counted as a failing grade.
- Three unexcused tardies will be counted as one unexcused absence.
- All Admit slips for the tardies or absences should bear the signature of the proper school authority.
- Report to class in the prescribed uniform.
- Take off cap and/or dark glasses. No mp3 players or radios allowed.
- Lift desks/chairs when getting together for group activities.
- At the end of a class period, replace chairs in the manner they were found.
- No eating or chewing gum allowed in class.
- Remove garbage from inside desks at the end of the class period.
- Foul language, cheating, disorderliness, and any type of misconduct will not be tolerated.
- Be courteous, cheerful, cooperative, caring of others, attentive, and respectful at all times.
- Raise your hand to be acknowledged before speaking.

Appendix C

Monthly Attendance and Grade Report

St. Cedar High School
Riverdale #2
Stormhill, Bonanza, UG 1111
November 30, 1991

Dear Parent,

This is your child's weekly attendance and grade report for the week of (place dates here).

ATTENDANCE:
Your child was absent on the dates indicated:
Language Arts:
Social Studies:
Math:
Science:

Your son/daughter earned the following grades for week (place dates here):

If you wish to have a conference with your child's teacher, please complete the request form for *Parent-Teacher Conferences* and mail it to Dr. L. Garrad at the address that appears at the top of the form. You may also send the form with your child.

Sincerely,
The Tenth Grade Team

Appendix D

Request Form for a Parent-Teacher Conference

Educators
St. Cedar High School
Riverdale #2
Stormhill, Bonanza, UG 1111

Date of receipt: _____
Date of return: _____

Dear Team:

I have received my son/daughter's weekly attendance and grade report. I can be easily contacted at this phone number _____.
My correct address is: (Indicate any changes in your address)
　　I am requesting a conference to discuss the following:

My selected meeting time is (choose one):

　　_____ Period 3 (9:55 am)
　　_____ Period 7 (2:10 pm)

Please print and sign the form and either mail or return to Dr. L. Garrad, Team Facilitator.

_____
　　Print Name

_____
　　Signature

If you have any questions, please call us at 294/913-6742. Before you submit this form, please make a copy.

Appendix E

Collaborating with the Guidance Department

ILT
St. Cedar High School
Riverdale #2
Stormhill, Bonanza, UG 1111

To: Dr. B. Chell, Chair
    Guidance Department
From: Dr. L. Garrad, Team Facilitator
Date: October 4, 1991
Re: Career Opportunities/Colleges

Utilizing a survey developed by Gordon Vars, the educators of ILT codified students' responses to the question what do they see themselves doing in ten years. As head of the guidance department, we are requesting your assistance in identifying individuals in the community who are in the professions selected by the students. We would like to invite them to our career day activity that is being planned for December. We are particularly interested in the following professions:

- Air Force (Pilot)
- Law Enforcement
- Business Owner
- Secretary
- Mechanic
- Manager (Any field)
- Educator
- Computer Engineer
- Cosmetologist
- Doctor/Physician
- Office Procedures
- Working with the disabled

A component of the individual presentations should be information on educational requirements and what the job entails.

The monthly career activity schedule for the rest of the school year will be released in January.

We await your response, thank you.

Appendix F

Response from the Guidance Department

St. Cedar High School
Riverdale #2
Stormhill, Bonanza, UG 1111

To: Dr. L. Garrad
From: Dr. B. Chell, Chair
   Guidance Department
Date: October 7, 1991
Re: Career Opportunities/Colleges

As per your request dated October 4, 1991, the guidance department is happy to comply. For your records, the following counselors have agreed to be responsible for the areas indicated below:

Mr. M.:
Air Force
Law Enforcement
Business Owner
Mechanic
Cosmetologist
Office Procedures
Working with the disabled

Mr. T.:
Managers
Doctor/Physician
Educator
Computer Engineer

Please do not hesitate to contact me if we can be of further assistance.

Appendix G

Career Program Presentation Schedule

St. Cedar High School
Riverdale #2
Stormhill, Bonanza, UG 1111

To: Mr. M. Fox, Counselor
    Mr. T. Lang, Counselor
From: Dr. L. Garrad, Team Facilitator
Date: October 14, 1991
Re: Career Program Presentation Schedule

Thank you for volunteering your time to assist the students of the Integrated Learning Team (ILT). At a time when it is difficult to set achievable goals, exposing the students to their careers of interest is indeed an act of nurturing growth and direction.

    The schedule for the areas you agreed to coordinate is as follows:

December 2, 1991

Air Force	07:45–09:50
Law Enforcement	09:00–12:00
Business Owner	12:05–02:05

December 3, 1991

Secretary/Office Procedures	07:45–09:50
Mechanic	09:00–12:05
Cosmetologist	12:00–02:05

December 4, 1991

Working with the Disabled	07:45–9:50
Educator	09:00–12:00

Computer Engineer	12:05–02:05

December 5, 1991

Manager	07:45–09:50
Doctor	09:00–12:05

Allow me to reiterate your role. We welcome your assistance in planning this event, and identifying presenters in the above-mentioned fields. In addition, if you could do a brief presentation on which colleges are best suited for these professions we would be extremely grateful.

Our goal is to have the students develop a portfolio for the profession of their choice, which will include the colleges that best match the students' profiles. The memo (see appendix F) from Dr. L. is attached as well as the letter (see appendix I) that will be sent to the presenters. Room numbers will be added in the final correspondence.

Appendix H

Thank You Letter to Counselors

Integrated Learning Team
St. Cedar High School
Riverdale #2
Stormhill, Bonanza, UG 1111

December 9, 1991
Dear (Counselor):

The students and teachers of the Integrated Learning Team wish to express their appreciation for the time and energy you expended to make their career event a success. The uniqueness of the activity is that the careers discussed were ones in which the students had indicated an interest. Thus the presentations were of a personalized nature. Our group is small but our hearts are big. Once again, our heartfelt thanks for your unwavering assistance in identifying and contacting the presenters.

Sincerely,
    Dr. L. Garrad
    On behalf of the Integrated Learning Team
    cc: Mr. J. N. Principal
    Asst. Principals

Appendix I

Thank-You Letter to Presenters

Integrated Learning Team
St. Cedar High School
Riverdale #2
Stormhill, Bonanza, UG 1111

December 9, 1991
Dear (Presenter):

On behalf of the students of the Integrated Learning Team, we would like to thank you for spending quality time with us to share important information on your chosen career with the students. We apologize for the few students who did not attend. Such behavior is exactly the kind we are hoping to reconcile. Again we thank you as we hold firmly to the belief that in education we strive to save at least one starfish at a time.

Sincerely,

Dr. L. Garrad, on behalf of the Integrated Learning Team

cc: Mr. J. N., Principal
    Asst. Principals

Appendix J

Youth Multi-Service Center

YMSC

The Youth Multi-Service Center (YMSC) truly lives up to its name. YMSC provides a wide range of services to youth.

Homework assistance, tutoring, information about careers, or simply someone to talk to about problems are just a few of the services that YMSC provides.

Services offered include:

- PRE-EMPLOYMENT ATTITUDINAL SKILLS TRAINING INNO-VATION
    For dropouts, academic and employment skills training offered two times a year
- SUPPLEMENTAL EDUCATION SUPPORT
    Providing supportive services to students throughout the school year territory-wide
- YOUTH REHABILITATION CENTER (YRC)
    Providing incarcerated youth an opportunity to develop vocational skills that can be pursued upon release
- YOUTH DEVELOPMENT PROJECT
    Providing counseling sessions and motivational groups throughout the community
- SUBSTANCE ABUSE AND SEX EDUCATION
    Educating youth about the dangers of drugs and early sex
- COLLEGE PLACEMENT AND REFERRAL SERVICE
    Giving youth new opportunities to go to college
- YOUTH AND FAMILY COUNSELING
    Being available when a crisis tears a family apart

So if you need help, call 779-1009 or drop by the Youth Multi-Service Center.

Appendix K

Extra Credit Information

EARN EXTRA CREDIT POINTS EACH DAY OF THE WEEK

Monday: Newspaper summary
Points for this activity can be earned by preparing a summary of a newspaper article dealing with current world affairs. The article must be neatly pasted on a blank sheet of paper above the summary.
    Value: 25 points

Tuesday: Early Bird Special
The first student to arrive to class receives the extra points.
    Value: 5 points

Wednesday: Whiz Kid
Start the day with a question about curricula and extra curricula information. Any student answering correctly receives the points.
    Value: 35 points

Thursday: Weekly Journal
Selecting a topic of your choice, write one paragraph. The paragraph must have a main idea and supporting information. The use of appropriate writing skills is a must.
    Value: 50 points

Friday: Perfect Attendance
All students who have perfect attendance for the week receive extra points. Perfect attendance includes being to class on time.
    Value: 5 points

Days	Date/ Points	Date/ Points	Date/ Points	Date/ Points	Totals
Monday					
Tuesday					
Wednesday					
Thursday					
Friday					
Total					

Student Name: _____

Appendix L

Two-Month Evaluation Results

TOP RESPONSES TO STUDENT SURVEY

ILT is working; more positive about school
Don't like constant communication with parents
Don't like reports sent home; should be shared only with students

STAFF RESPONSES

Data collection and record keeping essential to making decisions on instruction
Collaborative planning and planning time supports professional growth
Parent involvement can work

Appendix M

Budget for Integrated Learning Teams

SY 1991–1992

Expenses	In-Kind	Cost	Budgeted Amount	Balance
			$20,000	
Bay Area Writing Workshops		$6,350		$13,650
Swann Workshops (SAT prep John Swann, Dayton Public Schools)		$1,235		$12,415
Integrating the Curriculum — Robin Fogarty		$3,491.43		$8,923.57
McCarthy 4MAT System		$2,235.48		$6,688.09
Michael Serra, Paper Geometry		$1,674.95		$5,013.14
Sandra Parks		$2,324.33		2,688.81
SAT Skills, Lynn Blanton (St. Croix)	$3,565.24			
Portfolio Assessment, Sara Mayhurt (St. Croix)	$3,545.42			
Printing Services	$6,661.20			
*Pretest		$4,830.00		−$2,141.29
Post test (Title 1)	$4,830.00			
Total Expenditure		**$22,141.19**		
Total In-Kind	**$18,601.86**			
Deposit from donations and sales			$2,141.29	$0.00

*parents paid

Bibliography

Ames, C., M. Khoju, and T. Watkins. (1993, March). *Parent Involvement: The Relationship between School-to-Home Communication and Parents' Perceptions and Beliefs*. Report number 15. Baltimore: Center on Families, Communities, Schools, and Children's Learning.

Aronson, E., N. Blaney, C. Stephan, J. Skies, and M. Snapp. (1978). *The Jigsaw Classroom*. Beverly Hills, CA: Sage Publications.

Barth, R. (1979). "Home-Based Reinforcement of School Behavior: A Review and Analysis." *Review of Educational Research* 3(49), 436–58.

Bauch, J. P. (1990, Spring). "Touch 1 for Improved Parent Educator Contact." *School Safety*, 25–27.

Becher, R. (1984). *Parental Involvement: A Review of Research and Principles of Successful Practice*. Washington, DC: National Institute of Education.

Bednar, R. L., and S. L. Weinberg. (1970). "Ingredients of Successful Programs for Underachievers." *Journal of Counseling Psychology* 17(1), 1–7.

Bellanca, J., and R. Fogarty. (1991). *Blueprints for Thinking in the Cooperative Classroom*. 2nd ed. Palatine, IL: Skylight Publishing.

Bernard, B. (1991, August). "Fostering Resiliency in Kids: Protective Factors in the Family, School, and Community." Paper presented at the Northwest Regional Educational Laboratory, Portland, OR.

Bloom, B. S. (1956). *Taxonomy of Educational Objectives*. New York: David Mackay.

Bloom, B. S., and E. D. Hirsch. (1987). *The Closing of the American Mind*. New York: Simon & Schuster.

Borland, J. H. (1986). "The Interdisciplinary Concept Model: Theory and Practice." *Gifted Child Quarterly* 30(4), 159–63.

Brady, M. (1989). *What's Worth Teaching?: Selecting, Organizing, and Integrating Knowledge*. Albany: State University of New York Press.

Brandt, R. (1998). *Powerful Learning*. Alexandria, VA: Association for Supervision and Curriculum Development.

Brophy, J. (1981, Spring). "Teacher Praise: A Functional Analysis." *Review of Educational Research* 51(1), 5–32.

Bruer, J. T. (1993). *Schools for Thought: A Science of Learning in the Classroom*. Cambridge, MA: MIT Press.

Buck Institute for Education. (2003). *Project-Based Learning Handbook: A Guide to Standards-Focused Project Based Learning for Middle and High School Teachers*. Novato, CA: Buck Institute for Education. Introduction chapter free to download at www.bie.org/tools/handbook.

Bullock, T. L., M. D. Gall, J. P. Gall, and D. R. Jacobson. (1990). *Tools for Learning: A Guide to Teaching Study Skills*. Alexandria, VA: ASCD.

Calfee, R., and C. Wadleigh. (1992). "How Project READ Builds Inquiring Schools." *Educational Leadership* 50(1), 28–32.

Cannady, L. C., and M. Rettig. (1995). *Block Scheduling: A Catalyst for Change in High School*. Princeton, NJ: Eye on Education.

Chang, H. (2010, September 15). "Five Myths about School Attendance." *Education Week*, p. 29.

Chavkin, N. F. (1989). "Low-Income Parents' Attitudes toward Parent Involvement in Education. *Journal of Sociology and Social Welfare* 3, 17–28.

Clark, R. M. (1988, Winter). "Parents as Providers of Linguistic and Social Capital." *Educational Horizons* 66, 93–95.

Clark, R. M. (1991). "Social Identity, Peer Relations, and Academic Competence of African-American Adolescents." *Education and Urban Society* 24(1), 41–52.

Clark, R. M. (1993). "What Research Says about the Importance of School-Home Communication."

Coalition of Essential Schools. "CES Affiliates."www.essentialschools.org/affiliates. Accessed December 21, 2011.

Coleman, J. S. (1987, August/September). "Families and Schools." *Educational Researcher* 6, 32–38.

Comer, J. P. (1986). "Parent Participation in Schools." *Phi Delta Kappan* 67(6), 442–46.

Common Core State Standards. (2011). www.corestandards.org.

Cooper, H. (1989). *Homework*. New York: Longman.

Costa, A. L. (1991). *The School as a Home for the Mind*. Palatine, IL: Skylight Publishing.

Courrege, D. (2011). "How Two Rural Schools Prepare Kids for College Part 1." *Rural Education* (blog), *Education Week*, July 29, 2011. Published in ASCD SmartBrief August 2, 2011.

Davies, D. J., P. Burch, and V. R. Johnson. (1992). *A Portrait of Schools Reaching Out: Report of a Survey on Practices and Policies of Family-Community-School Collaboration (No. 1)*. Baltimore: Center on Families, Communities, Schools, and Children's Learning.

Davies, D. J., P. Burch, and V. R. Johnson. (1996). *Partnerships for Student Success*. Boston: Center on Families, Communities, Schools and Children's Learning.

DeVries, D., and K. Edwards. (1973). "Learning Games and Student Teams: Their Effects on the Classroom Process." *American Educational Research Journal* 10(4), 307–18.

Donnelly, M. (1978). *At-Risk Students*. Report number 21. Eugene, OR: ERIC Clearinghouse on Educational Management. Eric Digest Series No. 292172.

Donohue-Smith. M. (2006, April 7). "There Is Such a Thing as a Stupid Question." *The Chronicle Review*, p. 1.

Eastwood, K., and K. Seashore Louis. (1992). "Restructuring That Lasts: Managing the Performance Dip." *Journal of School Leadership* 2(2), 213–24.

Elvin, L. (1977). *The Place of Common Sense in Educational Thought*. London: Unwin Educational Books.

Epstein, J. L. (1984). "Effects of Educator Practices on Parent Involvement: Change in Student Achievement in Reading and Math." Paper presented at the American Educational Research Association.

Epstein, J. L. (2001). *School, Family, and Community Partnerships: Preparing Educators and Improving Schools*. Boulder, CO: Westview Press.

Erikson, E. H. (1963). *Childhood and Society*. 2nd ed. New York: W.W. Norton.

Feuerstein, R. (1980). *Instrumental Enrichment*. Baltimore: University Park Press.

Fogarty, R. (1991). *The Mindful School: How to Integrate the Curricula*. 2nd ed. Palatine, IL: Skylight Publishing.

Fruchter, N., A. Galleta, and J. L. White. (1992). *New Directions in Parental Involvement*. New York: Academy for Educational Development.

Fullan. M. (2011). *Change Leader: Learning to Do What Matters Most*. San Francisco: Jossey-Bass.

Gall, M. D. (1975). *The Effects of Educator Use of Questioning Techniques on Student Achievement and Attitude*. San Francisco: Far West Laboratory for Educational Research.

Gall, M. D., J. P. Gall, and D. R. Jacobson. (1990). *Tools for Learning: A Guide to Teaching Study Skills*. Alexandria, VA: Association for Supervision and Curriculum Development.

Gallup, G. H. (1981, Spring). "The 13th Annual Gallup Poll of the Public's Attitudes toward Public Schools." *Phi Delta Kappan* 62, 33–47.

Glasgow, N. A., and P. J. Whitney (2008). *What Successful Schools Do to Involve Families: 55 Partnership Strategies*. Thousand Oaks, CA: Corwin Press.

Goodlad, J. I. (1984). *A Place Called School: Prospects for the Future*. New York: McGraw Hill.

Hall, E. (1983). "A Conversation with Erik Erikson." *Psychology Today* 17(6), 22, 24–30.

Henderson, A. (1987). *The Evidence Continues to Grow: Parental Involvement Improves Student Achievement*. Columbia, MD: National Committee for Citizens in Education.

Hoover-Dempsey, K. V., O. C. Bassler, and J. Brissie. (1987). "Parent Involvement: Contributions of Educator Efficacy, School Socioeconomic Status, and Other School Characteristics." *American Educational Research Journal* 24(3), 417–35.

Jacobs, H. H. (1989). "The Growing Need for Interdisciplinary Curriculum Content." In *Interdisciplinary Curriculum: Design and Implementation*, edited by H. H. Jacobs, 1–11. Alexandria, VA: Association for Supervision and Curriculum Development.

Jacobs, H. H. (2010). *Curriculum 21: Essential Education for a Changing World*. Alexandria, VA: Association for Supervision and Curriculum Development.

Jayanthi, M., J. S. Nelson, V. Sawyer, W. D. Bursuck, J. Epstein, and H. Michael. (1995). "Homework Communication Problems among Parents, Classroom Educators, and Special Education Educators: An Exploratory Study." *Remedial and Special Education* 16(2), 102–16.

Johnson, D. W., and R. Johnson. (1984). *Circles of Learning: Cooperation in the Classroom*. Alexandria, VA: Association for Supervision and Curriculum Development.

Johnson, D. W., and R. Johnson. (1998). "Cooperative Learning, Values, and Culturally Plural Classrooms." In *Values, the Classroom, and Cultural Diversity*, edited by M. Leicester, C. Modgil, and S. Modgil. London: Cassell PLC.

Joseph, J. M. (1994). *The Resilient Child: Preparing Today's Youth for Tomorrow's World*. New York: Plenum Press.

Joyce, B., and B. Showers. (1995). *Student Achievement through Staff Development*. 2nd ed. White Plains, NY: Longman.

Kirscenbaum, D. S., and M. G. Perri. (1982). "Improving Academic Competence in Adults: A Review of Recent Research." *Journal of Counseling Psychology* 29, 76–94.

Kline, P., and B. Saunders. (2010). *Ten Steps to a Learning Organization*. 2nd ed. Salt Lake City, UT: Great River Books.

Kounin, J. (1970). *Discipline and Group Management in Classrooms*. Huntington, NY: R. E. Krieger.

Krasnow, J. (1990). *Building Parent-Teacher Partnerships: Prospects from the Perspective of the Schools Reaching Out Project*. Boston: Boston Institute for Responsive Education, Schools Reaching Out Project.

Lenz, B. K., and G. R. Alley. (1983). *The Effects of Advanced Organizers on the Learning and Retention of Learning Disabled Adolescents within the Context of a Cooperative Planning Model*. Final research report submitted to the U.S. Department of Education, Office of Special Education, Washington, DC.

Lieberman, A., and L. Miller. (1999). *Teachers Transforming Their World and Their Work*. New York: Teachers College Press; Alexandria, VA: ASCD.

National Commission on Excellence in Education. (1983). *A Nation at Risk: The Imperative for Educational Reform*. www2.ed.gov/pubs/NatAtRisk/index.html. Accessed July 2009.

Mathews, J. (2009). *Work Hard. Be Nice: How Two Inspired Teachers Created the Most Promising Schools in America*. Chapel Hill, NC: Algonquin Books of Chapel Hill.

Meadows, G. J., V. Shaw-Taylor, and F. Wilson. (1993). "Through the Eyes of Parents." *Educational Leadership* 2(51), 31–34.

Melnick, S. A. (1990, Spring). *Assessing Parents' Attitudes toward School Effectiveness*. Paper presented at the Annual Meeting of the American Educational Research Association, Boston.

Moles, O. C. (1990). *Disadvantaged Parents' Participation in their Children's Education*. Washington, DC: Office of Educational Research and Improvement, U.S. Department of Education.

Moles, O. C., et al. (1993). *Building School-Family Partnerships for Learning: Workshops for Urban Educators.* Washington, DC: Office of Educational Research and Improvement, U. S. Department of Education.

Morrissey, M. S., and C. D'Ette. (2000). "Creating and Sustaining a Professional Learning Community: Actions and Perceptions of Leadership." Paper presented at AERA, April 26, 2000, Southwest Educational Development Laboratory.

Mullen, B. (1988, April). "Evaluation of Tips-Math in Creve Coeur Schools (IL)." Paper presented at a meeting of the American Educational Research Association, Washington, DC.

"Perfect Attendance Central." *Imagestuff.com.* www.imagestuff.com/programs/perfattend. Accessed March 4, 2010.

Perkins, D. N. (1989). "Selecting Fertile Themes for Integrated Learning." In *Interdisciplinary Curriculum: Design and Implementation,* edited by H. H. Jacobs, 67–76. Alexandria, VA: Association for Supervision and Curriculum Development.

Posner, M. I., and M. E. Raichle. (1997). *Images of Mind.* New York: Scientific American Library.

Pribram, K. (1974). *Holonomy and Structure in Organization of Perception.* Stanford, CA: Stanford University Press.

Reeves, D. (1996). *Making Standards Work.* Denver, CO: Center for Performance Assessments.

Sasser, K. (1991). "Parent Involvement in Schools: Reluctant Participants Do Not Equal Uninterested Parents." Paper presented at the Annual Meeting of the Mid-South Educational Research Association, Lexington, KY.

Scott-Jones, D. (1991). "Adolescent Childbearing: Risks and Resilience." *Education and Urban Society* 24(1), 53–64.

Secretary's Commission on Achieving Necessary Skills. (1991). "What Work Requires of Schools." *SCANS Report for America 2000.*

Seligman, M. (1991). *Learned Optimism.* New York: Alfred A. Knopf.

Senge, P. (1990). *The Art and Practice of the Learning Organization.* New York: Doubleday Currency.

Senge, P., N. Cambron-McCabe, T. Lucas, B. Smith, J. Dutton, and A. Kleiner. (2000). *Schools that Learn: A Fifth Discipline Fieldbook for Educators, Parents, and Everyone Who Cares about Education.* New York: Doubleday/Currency.

Shanker. A. (1979). *Where We Stand (21).* Washington, DC: American Federation of Educators.

Sizer, T. (1984). *Horace's Compromise: The Dilemma of the American High School.* Boston: Houghton Mifflin Company.

Slavin, R. (1974). *The Effects of Teams in Teams-Games-Tournament on the Normative Climates of Classrooms.* Baltimore: Center for Social Organization of Schools, John Hopkins University.

Smith, S. C., and J. J. Scott. (1990). *The Collaborative School: A Work Environment for Effective Instruction.* Eugene, OR: ERIC Clearinghouse on Educational Management, University of Oregon. ERIC Document Reproduction Service NO. ED316918.

Snow, D. R. (2005). *Classroom Strategies for Helping At-Risk Students.* Aurora, CO: Mid-continent Research for Education and Learning.

Sparks, D. (2001). "Why Change Is So Challenging for Schools." *Journal of Staff Development* 22(3), 42–47.

Sparks, D. (2007). *Leading for Results: Transforming Teaching, Learning, and Relationships in Schools.* Thousand Oaks, CA: Corwin Press.

Stigler, J. W., and J. Hiebert. (1999). *The Teaching Gap.* New York: Free Press.

Swick, K. J. (1988). "Parent Efficacy and Involvement: Influences on Children." *Childhood Education* 65, 37–42.

Teacher Leader Consortium. (2011). "Teacher Leader Standards." NJ: Educational Testing Service.

U.S. Department of Education. (1986). *A Nation at Risk.* Washington, DC: Government Printing Office.

U.S. Department of Labor. (1991). *What Work Requires of Schools: A SCANS Report for America 2000 (The Secretary's Commission on Achieving Necessary Skills).* Washington, DC: U.S. Government Printing Office. www.uni.edu/darrow/frames/scans.html.

Vars, G. F. (1978). *Interdisciplinary Teaching in the Middle Grades.* Columbus, OH: National Middle School Association.

Vygotsky, L. (1978). *Mind in Society: The Development of High Psychological Processes.* Edited by V. John-Steiner, M. Cole, S. Scribner, and E. Souberman. Cambridge, MA: Harvard University Press.

Walberg, H. J., R. A. Paschal, and T. Weinstein. (1985). "Homework's Powerful Effects on Learning." *Educational Leadership* 42(7), 76–79.

Wiggins, G., and J. McTighe. (2005). *Understanding by Design.* Upper Saddle River, NJ: Prentice Hall.

Zimmerman, B. J. (1986). "Development of a Structured Interview for Assessing Student Use of Self-Regulated Learning Strategies." *American Educational Research Journal* 23, 614–628.

Zimmerman, B. J., A. Bandura, and M. Martinez-Pons. (1992). "Self-Motivation for Academic Attainment: The Role of Self-Efficacy Beliefs and Personal Goal Setting." *American Educational Research Journal* 29(3), 663–76.

Index

academic objectives, 31
academic skills: cooperative learning for, 39; library for, 38, 54; Socratic method for, 39; time-management for, 38
accountability, 21
American Youth Policy Forum, 56
ASCD. *See* Association of Supervision and Curriculum Development
assessment, 57, 81; academic objectives compared to instructional objectives in, 31; about attitudes, 32; baseline scores for, 45–46; budget for, 107; changes in, 65; continuous, 71, 81; data for, 11; departmental exams, 41, 45, 46; of impact, 105, 32, 45; of nonacademic goals, 11; objectives and, 11; of reform projects, 11; report cards as, 45–46; understanding about, 31; weekly progress reports as, 32–33; of writing, 30, 46
Association of Supervision and Curriculum Development (ASCD), 7–8
attendance, 1, 21; accountability for, 21; Early Bird program for, 103, 33, 42; ILT and, 53; ILT implementation and, 12, 13; incentives for, 103, 33, 33, 60; monthly report on, 87; of pure students, 53; school compared to ILT in, 53; of un-pure students, 53
attitudes, 32, 69. *See also* belief systems
Average Yearly Progress (AYP), 65

Bandura, Albert, 24
Bay Area Writing Project, 107, 24, 36
Bednar, R. L., 15
behavior, 36, 72; distractions and, 22; gang-related activities, 36;
instruction and, 22; research on, 22
belief systems: as challenges, 40–42; of team, 64; transformation of, 61
blog, 56
Bloom, Benjamin, 25–26, 27, 79
Borland, J. H., 31
Brandt, Ron, 11, 12, 62
Bruce, Joyce, 75
Bruer, John, 24
Budget for Integrated Learning Teams, 107
Bullock, 38
business partnerships, 33, 36, 55

Cannady, Robert, 13
careers, 28; assemblies on, 45; cooperative learning for, 39; employability, 6; incentives for, 33; instruction and, 10; job program for, 62; of parents, 35; social skills and, 54; student survey and, 8. *See also* college fairs
career day: aid proposal for, 91; response about, 93; schedule for, 95–96; thanking counselors for, 97; thanking presenters for, 99. *See also* college fairs
Career Program Presentation Schedule, 95–96
celebrations, 23
challenges: belief systems as, 40–42; policies as, 40
Chang, Hedy, 13
Chronicle Review, 25
Circles of Learning: Cooperation in the Classroom (Johnson and Johnson), 39
classes: as laboratories, 59; movement between, 20–21, 41; requirements for, 85; rules for, 85; size of, 20, 41. *See also* school; un-pure students

Classroom Strategies for Helping At-risk Students (Snow), 16

Class Rules, 85

Collaborating with the Guidance Department, 91

collaboration, 73, 80; cost-effectiveness of, 61; with guidance department, 91, 93, 15, 55; students and, 75; for team, 3, 21, 59, 64, 73; technology and, 65; time for, 13, 14, 21

college credits, 56

college fairs, 15, 20, 36, 60

Common Core State Standards, 9, 66, 80

communication, 43; articulation as, 38; with parents, 87, 89, 34, 34, 63. *See also* writing

community: PLCs, 75, 79; school culture as, 8, 17, 74

community service: for National Honor Society, 61; Peer Leaders for, 35, 61; pollution and, 29

compensation, 14, 41

competition, 60

conflict resolution, 27

content: Bloom's taxonomy and, 25–26; homework and, 14; mastery of, 31; note-taking and, 24; skills and, 27–31

Costa, Arthur, 6, 12, 26, 57

costs, 14, 37, 41, 61; budget, 107; funding, 42, 72, 80; prom funds in, 37–38

Council of Chief State School Officers, 9

counseling, 15; YMSC for, 101, 36, 61. *See also* career day

Courrege, Diette, 56

culture, 61–62; diversity in, 23. *See also* school culture

curriculum, 9, 26, 65–66; ASCD for, 7–8; Bloom's taxonomy for, 25–26; note-taking in, 24; relevance of, 8, 18, 23, 58, 80; SCANS in, 9

departmental exams, 41, 45, 46

D'Ette, 75

DeVries, David, 31

Donohue-Smith, Maureen, 25

Early Bird program, 103, 33, 42

Eastwood, Kenneth W., 75

Education Leadership, 12

Education Week, 56

Edutopia, 80

Edwards, Keith, 31

Elvin, Lionel, 19

employability, 6

enrollment distribution, 47, 48

environment, receptivity of, 66

Epstein, Joyce, 16

Erikson, Erik, 8, 11

Extra Credit Innovation, 103–104

faculty, 40, 64, 65; decision-making by, 75; principal compared to, 40–42. *See also* team

Focus 27, 72

Fogarty, Robin, 107, 9–10, 21, 26

Glasgow, Neal, 16

goals, 58, 60, 76; nonacademic, 11, 15, 55; thinking as, 26

grade distribution, 50; in language arts, 49; in math, 48, 49, 51, 52; in science, 49, 52, 54; in social studies, 49, 51, 52; team confidence related to, 64; in un-pure students (two-classes), 49, 53, 54; in un-pure students (three-classes), 48–49, 51

grade report, 87

Group Expectations Letter to Parents, 83

guidance department, 91, 93, 15, 55. *See also* career day; counseling

health, 23, 62

Hiebert, James, 75

Hirsch, E. D., 27

homework: completion rates of, 54, 63; content and, 14; parents and, 63; policy on, 14, 20, 40, 60

ILT. *See* Integrated Learning Teams

ILT implementation, 42–43; attendance and, 12, 13; block scheduling in, 13, 18; brain-stormed list for, 12–13; compensation for, 14; conditions for, 12–17; counseling in, 15;

justification for, 15; life skills and, 13; sequencing in, 14; stakeholders in, 15–16

impact, 46; assessment of, 105, 32, 45; on team, 55; on writing, 46. *See also* assessment

implementation: of reform projects, 81; of standards, 66. *See also* ILT implementation

incentives, 63; for attendance, 103, 33, 33, 60; competition as, 60; extra credit points as, 103–104, 33, 60; motivation and, 32, 60; weekly progress reports as, 32–33; writing as, 103, 103, 33

information, 5; for parents, 62

instruction, 9; behavior and, 22; careers and, 10; integration in, 9–10; structured tasks in, 24–25; thinking in, 9, 10. *See also* threaded model

instructional objectives, 31

Integrated Learning Teams (ILT), 107; attendance and, 53; cost-effectiveness of, 61; expectations for, 45; library and, 38, 54; name for, 17; school compared to, 51, 52, 52–53; 55; success of, 55, 64, 65; tutoring in, 35, 61. *See also* passing rates (ILT)

interdisciplinary teams, 66

international students, 6

interpersonal skills. *See* social skills

Jacobs, Heidi Hayes, 9, 10, 28, 32

Johnson, D. W., 39

Johnson, R., 39

Kay, Ken, 80

Kirscenbaum, D. S., 15

Kline, Peter, 12

language arts: grade distribution in, 49; passing rates (ILT) in, 47, 47–48; school compared to ILT, 51; school passing rates in, 51, 52, 55

library, 38, 54

Lieberman, Ann, 74

life skills, 54, 61; application forms in, 37; financial logs in, 37; ILT implementation and, 13; prom

funds in, 37–38; time-management skills in, 38

Louis, Karen Seashore, 75

Martinez-Pons, Manuel, 24

math: grade distribution in, 48, 49, 51, 52; paper geometry, 107, 21, 36; passing rates (ILT) in, 47, 47–48, 51, 52; school compared to ILT, 51; school passing rates in, 51, 52, 55

Mathews, Jay, 16

Miller, Lynne, 74

Monthly Attendance and Grade Report, 87

Morrison, Melanie, 75

motivation, 70, 73; incentives and, 32, 60

National Endowment of the Humanities, 42

National Governors Association, 9

National Honor Society, 61, 63

A Nation at Risk, 5, 6

nonacademic goals, 15, 55; assessment of, 11

parents, 14, 73; bilingual educators and, 35, 62; careers of, 35; communication with, 87, 89, 34, 34, 63; diversity and, 34, 35; homework and, 63; information for, 62; meeting with, 89, 34–35, 62–63; networking with, 35; notification to, 83, 34; partnerships with, 34–35, 54, 60; roles for, 16; Saturday Academies for, 34, 54, 63, 73; socioeconomics of, 1, 45; students' relationship with, 62; support from, 34, 35

Parks, Sandra, 107, 21

partnerships, 36; with businesses, 33, 36, 55; with consultants, 36; gang-related activities and, 36; in-school, 55, 80; with local teachers' union, 37; with parents, 34–35, 54, 60; with principal, 37; with school monitors, 36

passing rates (ILT): in language arts, 47, 47–48; in math, 47, 47–48, 51, 52; of pure students, 47, 48; in science,

47, 48, 50, 51, 54; in social studies, 47, 47–48, 49–50, 51, 52; of un-pure students, 47, 47–48, 48–50, 54; of un-pure students (one-class), 48, 50, 54; of un-pure students (two-classes), 48, 49–50; of un-pure students (three-classes), 47, 48

passing rates (school), 51, 52; in language arts, 51, 52, 55; in math, 51, 52, 55; in science, 51, 52, 55; in social studies, 51, 52, 55

PBL. *See* Project-Based Learning

Peer Leaders, 35, 61

Perri, M. G., 15

Phi Delta Kappan, 12

planning: for reform projects, 2, 2–3, 41, 58, 74, 81; time for, 41, 58, 74

PLCs. *See* professional learning communities

police officer, 36

policies, 56, 74; as challenges, 40; on homework, 14, 20, 40, 60; innovation and, 64; principal and, 60; program structure and, 20

Posner, M. I., 16

principal, 70; faculty compared to, 40–42; leadership of, 59–60, 81; partnership with, 37; policy and, 60; for reform project, 1–2; for shared leadership, 2, 59

professional development, 55, 73; avenues for, 12; consultants for, 36; Costa for, 12; as incentive, 63; need for, 74–75, 77, 81; time for, 21, 41

professional learning communities (PLCs), 75, 79

program structure, 27; class size in, 20, 41; feedback in, 20; movement between classes in, 20–21, 41; policy and, 20

progress reports: monthly, 87; report cards as, 45–46; weekly, 32–33

Project-Based Learning (PBL), 14

PSATs, 24

publications, 12

Puerto Ricans, 23

pure students, 47; attendance of, 53; correlation and, 48; passing rates of, 47, 48; percentage of, 47

Raichle, M. E., 16

reform projects, 37, 70, 74; assessment of, 11; context for, 1–2, 3; implementation of, 81; jealousy over, 64; planning for, 2, 2–3, 41, 58, 74, 81; PLCs for, 79; principal for, 1–2; terminology about, 71, 77; title for, 17; uncertainty about, 57; for whole child, 32, 54, 55, 66–67, 69. *See also* Integrated Learning Teams

Request Form for a Parent-Educator Conference, 89

research, 69; as basis, 17–18; on behavior, 22; cognitive dissonance and, 74; on counseling, 15; dated, 76; on discipline, 80; SCANS as, 5–6; standardized tests and, 42; team and, 105, 3, 58

resources, 5

Response from the Guidance Department, 93

Rettig, Michael, 13

Rose, David H., 76

rules, class, 85

safety, 1; location and, 41; police officer, 36; violence and, 36, 64

Santo Dominicans, 23

Saturday Academies, 34, 54, 63, 73

Saunders, Bernard, 12

SCANS. *See* Secretary's Commission on Achieving Necessary Skills Report

Scared Straight program, 36

scheduling, block, 13, 18, 66

school: attendance (ILT) compared to, 53; ILT compared to, 51, 52, 52–53, 55; language arts (ILT) compared to, 51; layout of, 13; math (ILT)compared to, 51; one class, 51–52; overcrowding in, 1; science (ILT) compared to, 51; social studies (ILT) compared to, 51; two classes, 52; violence at, 36, 64. *See also* passing rates (school); *specific subjects*

The School as a Home for the Mind (Costa), 6, 26, 57

school culture, 8, 16, 58, 61; as community, 8, 17, 74

school monitors, 36

science: grade distribution in, 49, 52, 54; passing rates (ILT) in, 47, 48, 50, 51, 54; school compared to ILT, 51; school passing rates in, 51, 52, 55

Secretary's Commission on Achieving Necessary Skills Report (SCANS), 5; in curriculum, 9; employability and, 6; on technology, 6

Showers, Beverly, 75

Sizer, Ted, 9, 13, 14, 25

skills, 52; content and, 27–31; in thinking, 26, 30. *See also* academic skills; life skills; social skills

Slavin, Robert, 31

Snow, David, 16

social outings, 23

social skills, 5, 8, 31, 38; articulation as, 38; careers and, 54; cooperative learning for, 39

social studies, 52; grade distribution in, 49, 51, 52; passing rates (ILT) in, 47, 47–48, 49–50, 51, 52; school compared to ILT, 51; school passing rates in, 51, 52, 55

Socratic method, 39

St. Cedar High School, 3

stakeholders, 72; buy-ins for, 16; in ILT implementation, 15–16; roles of, 15

standardized tests, 42, 65

Steinbeck, John, 29

Stigler, James, 75

students, 1, 64; celebrations for, 23; collaboration and, 75; confidence of, 62; health of, 23, 62; high-achieving, 24; international, 6; knowledge about, 22; novice compared to expert, 24; parents' relationship with, 62; pullouts of, 2; strategies about, 16–17; vulnerabilities of, 23. *See also* pure students; un-pure students

student survey, 105; careers and, 8; personal questions on, 7–8

Swann, John, 107, 24

teacher facilitator, 1, 22; background of, 2; role of, 61; Vars and, 7–8

Teacher Leader Standards, 61, 81

team, 16; as administrators, 41, 80; belief systems of, 64; as change agents, 16, 58, 59, 73; collaboration for, 3, 21, 59, 64, 73; confidence of, 64; for Erikson, 8; impact on, 55; interdisciplinary, 66; personal days for, 60; perspectives of, 2; research and, 105, 3, 58; selection of, 70; validity of, 57, 59, 75. *See also* Integrated Learning Teams; teacher facilitator

technology: collaboration and, 65; SCANS on, 6

Ten Steps to a Learning Organization (Kline and Saunders), 12

Terra Nova (standardized test), 8

Thank You Letter to Counselors, 97

Thank You Letter to Presenters, 99

thinking, 79; as goal, 26; in instruction, 9, 10; skills in, 26, 30

threaded model, 9–10, 18, 19; as meta-curricular approach, 26; thinking skills in, 26; unit structure in, 27

threaded model lesson design, 31, 58; conceptualization in, 26–27; court verdict example in, 30, 58; falling man example in, 30; without fragmentation, 27, 59; natural disaster example in, 29; pollution example in, 28–29

time: for collaboration, 13, 14, 21; for planning, 41, 58, 74; for professional development, 21, 41; standardized tests and, 42

time-management, 38

Title I funding, 42

truancy. *See* attendance

tutoring, 35, 61

Two-Month Evaluation Results, 105

UDL. *See* Universal Design for Learning

Understanding by Design, 65

Universal Design for Learning (UDL), 76

un-pure students: attendance of, 53;
    enrollment distribution of, 47, 48;
    passing rates (ILT) of, 47, 47–48, 48,
    48–50, 54
un-pure students (one-class):
    attendance of, 53; enrollment
    distribution of, 47, 48; passing rates
    (ILT) of, 48, 50, 54
un-pure students (two-classes):
    attendance of, 53; enrollment
    distribution of, 47, 48; grade
    distribution in, 49, 53, 54; passing
    rates (ILT) of, 48, 49–50
un-pure students (three-classes):
    attendance of, 53; enrollment
    distribution of, 47, 48; grade
    distribution in, 48–49, 51; passing
    rates (ILT) of, 47, 48

Vars, Gordon, 91, 7–8, 22
violence, 36, 64
Vygotsky, Lev, 24

Weinberg, S. L., 15
What's Worth Teaching, 9
*Work Hard. Be Nice: How Two Inspired
    Teachers Created the Most Promising
    Schools in America* (Mathews), 16
writing, 21; assessment of, 30, 46; Bay
    Area Writing Project, 107, 24, 36;
    impact on, 46; as incentive, 103, 103,
    33

Youth Multi-Service Center (YMSC),
    101, 36, 61

Zimmerman, Barry, 24, 38

About the Author

Rosalind LaRocque received her bachelor's degree from the University of the West Indies, Cave Hill, Barbados, where she graduated with honors. She began her teaching career in 1975, preparing students for the external General Certificate Exam set by Cambridge, and served briefly as an examiner for the Caribbean Examinations Council. In 1980, she obtained her MA in education from the University of the Virgin Islands, and by 2003 completed her PhD with Madison University.

As an educator in her homeland, the Common Wealth of Dominica, Mrs. LaRocque taught English and history and prepared students to take the GCE exams from England with much success. She later served as an examiner for the Caribbean Examinations Council, in Barbados.

Mrs. LaRocque's love for lifelong learning earned her several roles in the educational system. Before migrating to the Virgin Islands, she served as a member of the task force that wrote a site-based management proposal and the accompanying proposed contractual agreement between the government and AFT.

In St. Croix, Virgin Islands, where she spent some years of her teaching career, she served as a department chair and later went on to be one of the first five master teachers, under a union-district sponsored program. These roles exposed her to extensive training in research-based cognitive and instructional strategies as well as educational policy, systemic change, and reform. But her biggest role in education was working with adolescents. As a high school teacher, Mrs. LaRocque implemented activities she called the hidden curriculum to develop the "whole child."

Besides service-learning opportunities for students, and Saturday Academies working closely with the PTA, LaRocque enjoys the arts. At age thirteen, she established and choreographed dances for her group "La Belle Theatre." This group represented her country at the very first Caribbean cultural arts festival, Caribanna, held in Guyana in 1972. Dances performed by the group included modern, African, jazz, and traditional.

In the drama area, she played many lead roles in productions put on by the national drama organization and, as a teacher at her alma mater, she coordinated and directed many plays for the school's drama team. Mrs. LaRocque feels that the arts are an expression of who we really are. In St. Croix, she joined her students occasionally in their carnival efforts.

Mrs. LaRocque has received several certificates of appreciation and awards from her students, school, and community groups. She was the recipient of the Teacher of the Month and Teacher of the Year and has received awards for her contribution in education and community service from *Tomorrow's People* (*Community Service Award* in May 1990), from Rotary West in February 2000, and from the Dominica United Cultural Group in 2008 for outstanding contribution in the field of education.

Mrs. LaRocque has written several articles, including "Re-thinking Language Arts Instruction," *The Voice, Carnival* Magazine (1980); "Meeting Students' Needs," *CHS Echo*, the school newspaper; and was a contributing writer to the St. Croix BAWP Anthology, *Just Sitting There*. She also did a review for the *Daily News* (St. Thomas, VI) on Mark Sylvester's *The Road I Walk*. *Reform versus Dreams: Preventing Student Failure* (2012) is her first book.

Currently, Dr. LaRocque works in the Educational Issues Department of the American Federation of Teachers in Washington, DC, where she develops professional development courses and modules for educators.